D0778662

Holocaust Survivors and Immigrants

Late Life Adaptations

The Plenum Series on Stress and Coping

Series Editors: **Donald Meichenbaum**, *University of Waterloo, Waterloo, Ontario, Canada*

A CLINICAL GUIDE TO THE TREATMENT OF THE HUMAN STRESS
RESPONSE
Second Edition
George S. Everly, Jr. and Jeffrey M. Lating

CREATING A COMPREHENSIVE TRAUMA CENTER
Choices and Challenges
Mary Beth Williams and Lasse A. Nurmi

ETHNICITY, IMMIGRATION, AND PSYCHOPATHOLOGY
Edited by Ihsan Al-Issa and Michel Tousignant

HOLOCAUST SURVIVORS AND IMMIGRANTS
Late Life Adaptations
Boaz Kahana, Zev Harel, and Eva Kahana

INTERNATIONAL HANDBOOK OF HUMAN STRESS RESPONSE TO TRAUMA
Edited by Arieh Y. Shalev, Rachel Yehuda, and Alexander C. McFarland

INTERNATIONAL HANDBOOK OF MULTIGENERATIONAL LEGACIES
OF TRAUMA
Edited by Yael Danieli

THE MENTAL HEALTH CONSEQUENCES OF TORTURE
Edited by Ellen Gerrity, Terence M. Keane, and Farris Tuma

PSYCHOTRAUMATOLOGY
Key Papers and Core Concepts in Post-Traumatic Stress
Edited by George S. Everly, Jr. and Jeffrey M. Lating

STRESS, CULTURE, AND COMMUNITY
The Psychology and Philosophy of Stress
Steven E. Hobfoll

TOXIC TURMOIL
Psychological and Societal Consequences of Ecological Disasters
Edited by Johan M. Havenaar, Julie G. Cwikel, and Evelyn J. Bromet

TRAUMA, WAR, AND VIOLENCE
Public Mental Health in Socio-Cultural Context
Edited by Joop de Jong

A Continuation Order Plan is available for this series. A continuation order will bring delivery of
each new volume immediately upon publication. Volumes are billed only upon actual shipment.
For further information please contact the publisher.

Holocaust Survivors and Immigrants
Late Life Adaptations

Boaz Kahana
Cleveland State University Cleveland, Ohio

Zev Harel
Cleveland State University Cleveland, Ohio

and

Eva Kahana
Case Western Reserve University, Cleveland, Ohio

 Springer

Boaz Kahana
Department of Psychology
Cleveland State University
Cleveland, OH 44115
USA
b.kahana@csuohio.edu

Eva Kahana
Department of Sociology
Case Western University
Cleveland, OH 44106-7124
exk@po.cwru.edu

Zev Harel
School of Social Work
Cleveland State University
Cleveland, OH 44114
USA
zharel@csuohio.edu

Series Editors:
Donald Meichenbaum
University of Waterloo
Waterloo, ON, CANADA
N2L 3G1

Cover illustration: Cover design by Susanne Van Duyne (Trade Design Group)
Cover image by Getty Images, Inc.

ISBN-10: 0-387-22972-8   e-ISBN: 0-387-22973-6   Printed on acid-free paper.
ISBN-13: 978-0387-22972-0

Printed in the United States of America.   (TB/IBT)

9 8 7 6 5 4 3 2 1

springeronline.com

We dedicate this book to those who perished in the Holocaust and to those who survived to bear witness and to build new lives and to raise a new generation. We also dedicate this book to our parents and to our children, young adults whose achievements we are proud of and who cherish the values of their grandparents.

Contents

Acknowledgements

We are very grateful to all the respondents who willingly and openly shared their difficult life experiences, and enriched us with their wisdom. We would also like to acknowledge the assistance of Dr. Sarajane Brittis in developing the second chapter of the book, focusing on first-hand accounts of Holocaust survivors in our study. Ms. Gul Seckin provided valuable assistance with literature reviews and preparation of the manuscript. We are also appreciative of the excellent editorial assistance of Drs. Jane Brown, Cathie King, and graduate students who have worked with them on this project: Judith Harris, Diana Tascar, and Antje Daub.

Preface

The aim of this book is to review and describe the lives, memories and experiences of older adults who have endured extreme trauma as survivors of the Nazi Holocaust. Through systematically collected interviews with Holocaust survivors living in the United States, and those residing in Israel, we seek to understand adverse responses to the trauma as well as adaptations that facilitate healing, functioning and productive participation in society. Our study places responses and characteristics of survivors in the context of the lives of individuals with similar backgrounds who managed to escape Nazi occupied lands prior to the Holocaust.

The orientation of this book synthesizes several distinct but related traditions. Explicating our roots in each of these fields of scholarly inquiry should clarify the conceptual approaches we share throughout this book. Specifically our study derives its approaches from gerontological and life span developmental research, from traditional stress research, and from the emerging field of traumatology. In addition to being informed by the distinct conceptual and methodological approaches of these areas of inquiry, the broader disciplinary roots of the three co-authors span Psychology (Boaz Kahana), Social Work (Zev Harel), and Sociology (Eva Kahana). Our analyses reflect the theoretical approaches of the disciplines we represent to understand the individual, society, and the interactions between the two.

All three co-authors have been trained in the quantitative traditions of social science research, but also appreciate the contributions of qualitative understanding for providing the crucial integrative context in which quantitative data are embedded (Kahana, Kahana, & Riley, 1989). Boaz Kahana worked for many years as a clinical psychologist doing assessments and therapy with diverse patients including individuals who were exposed to trauma and who exhibited stress reactions. Zev Harel has been a clinical social worker, with experience ranging from children to the elderly, and with an interest in organizational factors in human services. Eva Kahana has been interested in society's role in predisposing individuals to victimization and shaping both personal and social responses to trauma (Kahana, 1992, Leviton, 1991).

In terms of their experiential backgrounds, the authors also bring a spectrum of personal orientations to this book. Boaz Kahana grew up in the United States, a child of immigrants from Palestine. Zev Harel is a survivor of three concentration camps, and Eva Kahana was a hidden child in Hungary during the Holocaust. The co-authors have collaborated in conducting studies in the field of gerontology before applying their interests in coping with stress in later life to the unique case of Holocaust survivors. The journey from an idea broached by Zev Harel to the Kahanas led to the first National Institutes of Health funded study of elderly Holocaust survivors, conducted in both Israel and the United States. Writing this book has been an immense personal growth experience for all three authors.

The book is based on an empirical investigation of 150 Holocaust survivors living in the United States and 150 survivors living in Israel. Two comparison groups of similar ethnic background were also studied, consisting of 150 prewar immigrants to the U.S. and 150 prewar immigrants to Israel. The book reports on quantitative as well as qualitative responses of participants in this research. The book has taken many years to write during which we have had to confront the stresses and triumphs of our own lives and our own aging. This same period also witnessed the coming of age of the field of traumatology and growing national and international attention to the Nazi Holocaust.

It has been a privilege to share this journey with each other and with colleagues around the world. One of the early meetings of the fledgling Society for Traumatic Stress Studies took place at Cleveland State University in 1986, and the first international meeting of hidden children of the Holocaust took place in New York in the Spring of 1991. The launching of our research project in Detroit coincided with the building of one of the first Holocaust memorials in the United States. The interest generated by the completion of the memorial contributed to increasing interest in participation in our study among Holocaust survivors.

At the outset of our study in 1982 there were almost no quantitative social science based studies of Holocaust survivors, and most of what was known was based on eye witness accounts (Bettelheim, 1943, Frankl, 1992) or reports of clinicians about survivor patients seeking their help (Krystal, 1968). As we place our findings in the context of the relevant literature, it is exciting to note that empirical studies of survivors have begun to emerge both in the United States and Israel, providing evidence of stress reactions as well as of strengths and resiliency among survivors. Our research stands, however, as unique in its dual focus on Holocaust survivors both in the United States and in Israel. As such, it provides an important basis for considering areas of comparability and divergences in the survivor experience in two major cultural contexts where Holocaust survivors have been studied. Furthermore, we are able to consider the experiences and late life functioning of survivors in comparison to elderly Jewish immigrants who came to the US or Israel prior to World War II.

The first chapter of this book describes the conceptual approaches employed in this book. It identifies and synthesizes gerontological and stress research traditions. It offers an overview of stress experiences, and coping mechanisms used by Holocaust survivors and immigrants in their adaptation to aging and to challenges of living in the United States and Israel.

The second chapter witten in collaboration with Sarajane Brittis, describes the stressors experienced and coping mechanisms utilized by Holocaust survivors during World War II. First, the chapter reviews anti-Semitic policies and practices engaged in by the Nazis and their collaborators. Second, the chapter offers first hand accounts by Holocaust survivors of the stressors endured in the different countries in Europe and the ways they managed to live through them. This chapter provides a glimpse into the lived experience of what is really meant by Holocaust as a stressor.

The third chapter provides an overview of experiences of survivors in their quest to establish new lives in the United States and Israel, in the aftermath of their war time experiences. It reviews responses of survivors to the challenges and opportunities they faced in the immediate post-war years, including obtaining support from organizations that aided survivors.

The fourth chapter provides a conceptual overview of the cumulative stresses faced by survivors, empirical evidence about early life crises and the various stressors experienced by Holocaust survivors and immigrants in both the United States and in Israel during the Holocaust, in the post war years and in the long term aftermath of their trauma.

The fifth chapter provides a conceptual overview and a systematic comparison of the physical health status of Holocaust survivors and immigrants in both the United States and Israel. It provides data on summary health measures as well as detailed information about specific health problems.

The sixth chapter provides a conceptual overview and a systematic comparison of the mental health of Holocaust survivors and immigrants in both the United States and Israel. It reviews empirical data comparing survivors and immigrants on indices of mental health including the Lawton Morale Scale, Symptom Checklist (SCL90) and a Traumatization Inventory.

The seventh chapter focuses on social integration. Specifically it compares survivors and immigrants in both countries on social roles and affiliations, social interaction and social support measures.

The eighth chapter considers the multiple predictors of psychological well-being in late life. We compare the predictors of high morale for survivors and immigrants in both the United States and Israel.

The ninth and last chapter provides a conceptual closure and offers suggestions for future research to improve our comprehension of stress, coping and adaptation among older trauma victims. It offers suggestions concerning professional efforts that aim to enhance adjustment of stress victims to challenges faced in late life. Finally, it focuses on collective memory and memorialization of this cataclysmic period of history.

REFERENCES

Bettelheim, B. (1943). Individual and mass behavior in extreme situations. *Journal of Abnormal and Social Psychology*, 38, 417–452.

Frankl, V.E. (1992). *Man's Search for Meaning: An Introduction to Logotherapy*. Boston, MA: Beacon Press.

Kahana, E. Kahana, B., Riley, K. (1989). Person-Environment Transactions Relevant to Control and Helplessness in Institutional Settings. In P.S. Fry (Ed.), *Psychological Perspectives of Helplessness and Control in the Elderly*, pp. 121–153. Oxford, England: North Holland.

Kahana, E. (1992). Stress Research and Aging: Complexities, Ambiguities, Paradoxes, and Promise. In M. Wykle, E. Kahana, & J. Kowal (Eds.), *Stress and Health Among the Elderly*, pp. 239–256. New York, NY: Springer Publishing Company.

Krystal, H. (Ed.) (1968). *Massive Psychic Trauma*. New York, NY: International University Press.

Leviton, D. (Ed.) (1991). *Horrendous Death and Health: Toward Action*. Washington DC: Hemisphere Publishing Corporation.

1

Placing Adaptation Among Elderly Holocaust Survivors in a Theoretical Context

This chapter sets the stage for a description of the lives and memories of older adults who experienced extreme trauma as survivors of the Nazi Holocaust. It also provides a systematic review of prior work on the effects of the Holocaust on survivors and their adaptation to challenges in the postwar years. In setting the stage for presenting our empirical findings, we provide an overview of the conceptual frameworks we relied on for understanding adaptation of Holocaust survivors and immigrants. We delineate concepts we found useful within the gerontological, general stress, and traumatic stress traditions.

GERONTOLOGICAL TRADITIONS

The research questions giving rise to the study, which comprises the core of our book, reflect the interests of gerontologists, life span developmental psychologists and life course sociologists who aim to understand late life adaptation in response to stressful situations that individuals endured earlier in their lives. The central questions are related to vulnerability or resiliency among individuals who endured extreme early trauma. As gerontologists, we were concerned with the excess burdens borne by older adults who generally experienced social role losses and who endured stressful life situations at a time when their resources and adaptive capacities may be diminished (Rosow, 1967; Kahana, Kahana, & Kinney, 1990). Gerontological interests have traditionally centered on late life self concepts, attitudes toward one's own aging, feelings about impending dependency and predictors

1

of psychological well being in the face of declining health and increasing vulnerability (Atchley & Baruch, 2004). More recently attention has also been directed at "successful aging" and "aging well" the consideration of productive roles and meaningful lives that many elderly persons succeed in maintaining well into old age (Kahana, Midlarsky, & Kahana, 1987; Kahana & Kahana, 2003).

We believe that studying older adults who are living independently in the community and who are dealing with the usual challenges of aging in the wake of having experienced extreme stress earlier in their lives, can provide fresh insights into the spectrum of responses to adaptive challenges of aging. The combination of antecedents and outcome variables we consider reflects orientations of gerontological researchers to understanding predictors of health and subjective well being in later life (Maddox, 2001; Lawton, 1983). Our empirical work thus compares elderly survivors and immigrants on physical and mental health outcomes. We also consider demographic and health related predictors of good quality of late life among the two groups of respondents.

TRADITIONS OF GENERAL STRESS RESEARCH

In an effort to understand successful and unsuccessful aging, gerontologists have often turned to the stress paradigm as the most useful conceptual framework of person environment transactions in later life (Pearlin, 1989). Having relied on the general stress paradigm in our earlier gerontological studies (Kahana & Kahana, 1998; Harel, Ehrlich, & Hubbard, 1990; Kahana, Kahana, & Young, 1987), we turned to this conceptualization as a basic framework for understanding adaptation of the elderly to extreme stress.

The general stress literature has typically focused on the adverse influences of recent life events on physical and mental health (Dohrenwend & Dohrenwend, 1984). In this literature, outcomes are primarily seen as a function of events experienced by an individual during the previous year. More recently, it has been recognized that chronic stressors, hassles, and social strains also have important outcomes (Kahana & Kahana, 1998). It is suggested that the different forms of stress, which individually affect well being, may also be interrelated and have synergistic effects on the person (Krause, 1991; Pearlin, 1989). Nevertheless, it is noteworthy that empirical studies of stress and aging are still anchored in the recent past, with only cursory attention given to the impact of early life stress on later life adaptation (Antonovsky, 1979).

Beyond the recognition that stress causes distress, publications in this area also focus on the role of social and psychological resources in buffering adverse stress effects (Pearlin, Menaghan, Lieberman, & Mullan, 1981; Wheaton, 1997). Our research incorporates traditions of stress research by considering the cumulative stresses endured by survivors, and by exploring the roles of both internal and external resources as buffering the adverse effects of trauma and attendant chronic stresses (Kahana & Kahana, 1998).

TRAUMATIC STRESS TRADITIONS

One of the hallmarks of war and other man-made disasters is the range and extensiveness of losses experienced by victims, and the occurrence of these losses outside the rubric of a normal social structure (Raphael, 1986). Certainly, survivors of the Holocaust experienced extreme losses. They were stripped of their social identities, lost close family members and friends, their jobs, their homes, and their homelands (Bauer & Rotenstreich, 1981).

It has been argued by stress researchers that the magnitude of stress experienced is a function of the perceived personal cost of failure (McGrath, 1970). In the aftermath of extreme trauma such as the Holocaust, personal costs associated with failure in life threatening situations may be exaggerated, whereas the costs in relation to normative (e.g., work related or financial) stresses may be minimized (Tanay, 2004). Such altered appraisals may account for observations of decreased reactivity to current stress among those who have experienced early trauma (Krell, 2001). As older adults progress from work to retirement, and the specter of frailty and mortality are more close at hand, old-old survivors may exhibit greater adverse reactions to all stress (Landau & Litwin, 2000).

Our ability to accurately observe long-term effects of traumatic stress is limited by selective attrition. Accordingly, the longer one waits to study survivors of great trauma, the more selective our samples are likely to be in the direction of the hardiest survivors. Not only has the 80-year-old Holocaust survivor lived through incredible atrocities but he or she has succeeded in growing old and sustaining the ability to function in the community far beyond a time which was normative for his or her cohort. Thus, it is likely that survivorship bias among the oldest group of survivors will mask the special problems survivors may encounter as they approach greater frailty. Therefore, estimates of problems experienced by this population that are based on studies of long term survivors will be conservative.

Furthermore, we must also keep in mind that those who are the oldest among the group of survivors were also those who experienced the trauma as adults. They may have been less vulnerable to some of the psychological insults endured than those in earlier and more formative stages of personality development (Goulet & Baltes, 1970).

TEMPORAL DIMENSIONS OF SURVIVORSHIP

Incorporation of a temporal element in considering post-traumatic stress reactions has generally been implicit rather than explicit. Clinicians have considered the impact of early trauma for adult development as pivotal for understanding post traumatic stress disorder (McCann & Pearlman, 1990). Such understanding has a long history in psychoanalytic formulations of trauma (Wilson, 1989). Empirical stress researchers, however, have only very recently noted the potential usefulness of considering past stress, current stress and anticipated future stress as determinants of current psychological well being (Caplan, 1989). Such temporal components have been related to a congruence based view of stress, which reflects expectations of fluctuating incongruence between environmental demands and personal capabilities (Kahana & Kahana, 1983). Elaborating on such a view, Caplan (1989) argues for considering the continuing influence of negative past life experiences and anticipation of future stresses along with current stresses as collectively shaping well-being outcomes.

Researchers have thus noted the importance of the time in one's life course when the traumatic stressor was experienced. Amir and Lev-Wisel (2003) argue that only within the past fifteen years has research recognized the differential psychosocial effects of the Holocaust on personality development. These effects vary according to the age at which trauma was experienced (Chaitin, 2003). For example, "attachment theory" emphasizes the importance of early relationships with parents and the ability to develop secure attachments to one's parents at a very young age (Cohen, Dekel, & Solomon, 2002). This human need to develop secure attachments and the accompanying feeling that one is loved, protected, and secure are crucial for development of feelings of self-worth, and for trusting relationships with other people (Lev-Wiesel, 2000). Child survivors of the Holocaust were often forced to be separated from their families, to live in hunger and cold. They had to find a way to survive without the support of adult human beings. This sense of "shattering" of the protective and safe world at a very early age unavoidably affected the personality development of young survivors (Sigal, 1998).

Amir and Lev-Wiesel (2003) found that some child survivors show heightened symptomatology on PTSD-related characteristics, such as depression and anxiety. They also found that child survivors who do not remember their parents' identity, or those who were given alternative identities so that they could not be identified as a Jew, have a diminished quality of life compared to the survivors who remember or who were able to keep their original identity.

Child survivors of the Holocaust may also experience difficulties in forming trusting relationships with other people in their social environment (Sadavoy, 1997). The experience of being taken away from their families and homes by strangers, observing torture and willful cruelty may create a deep crack in the inner psychological world of child survivors, especially regarding issues of trust. Kellerman (2001) also argues that experiencing man-made trauma at a very early age leaves indelible marks on the developing personality of the child. The "victim-mind set" developed at the time of trauma may continue to exist into adulthood and into later life leaving survivors with a constant feeling that they have to be watchful of others (Moskovitz, 2001). Moreover, this inability to form a trusting relationship with other people may be especially problematic in old age when survivors become physically frail and need the help of formal caregivers, e.g., physicians and nurses (Sadavoy, 1997).

SOCIAL SUPPORTS AND COPING STRATEGIES AS BUFFERS IN THE STRESS PARADIGM

Upon liberation, most survivors were physically exhausted, disease ridden individuals who were cut off from most human attachments (Hilberg, 1985). If they were to make it as human beings, they had to re-attach themselves to a social structure and work to re-establish a social identity. In undertaking our study, we were eager to learn from survivors about their healing journey and find out just how they accomplished the feat of becoming functioning members of society in the aftermath of the genocide and torture they endured (Kahana, Kahana, Harel & Rosner, 1988; Midlarsky, 2005). We provide a detailed discussion of the role of social supports in buffering stressors of early trauma in chapter seven.

Guidelines from the stress literature identify social supports and coping resources as the most well established buffers of stress that can diminish ill effects of trauma (Cobb, 1976; Antonucci, 1991; George, 1990). We were especially interested in considering the role of personal coping resources and strategies as factors which contribute to resilience subsequent to trauma (Krause, 1991).

There have been several prevalent and sometimes overlapping definitions of coping strategies presented in the literature. Billings and Moos (1982) distinguished active behavioral, active cognitive, and avoidance-oriented strategies as critical components, while Pearlin and Schooler

(1978) differentiated coping strategies that alter the situation, modify the meaning of the situation, or control the stress of the situation. Lazarus and Folkman (1984) proposed a bi-dimensional formulation distinguishing problem-focused and emotion-focused dimensions. Work by Kahana, Kahana, & Young (1987) on institutionalized elderly supported a tripartite view of coping including instrumental, affective, and avoidance-based strategies. Following these traditions, our research also explores the use of diverse coping strategies by Holocaust survivors and the immigrants they are being compared to.

Coping strategies may be distinguished from coping resources and are defined as specific responses or behaviors utilized by individuals when problem situations arise (Lazarus & Folkman, 1984). Regardless of their classification, coping strategies are widely recognized as important buffers between stressful life events and adverse mental or physical health sequelae. Interest in the construct is justified by documented associations between modes of coping with problem situations and a range of outcomes. Previous research has documented the usefulness of coping strategies in enhancing psychosocial well-being subsequent to institutional placement of the elderly (Kahana, Kahana, & Young, 1987) among caregivers of frail elderly (Stephens, Norris, Kinney & Ritchie, 1988), and in response to chronic strain with finances, parenting, and occupations (Pearlin et al., 1981).

In order to better understand the effectiveness of specific coping processes we must specify the adaptive tasks older persons are dealing with as well as situational constraints on their coping options. Thus, for example, an elderly person confronting stress created by loss of income due to retirement may not readily find new employment and hence, there are limits on specific instrumental actions he can take to increase his own income. Similarly, opportunities for asking for assistance may be limited for elderly who had lost sisters and brothers in the Holocaust or who migrated to lands distant from their siblings. Thus, the very losses in resources which are so apt to characterize old age can also serve to limit coping options available to the older person. Consequently, coping resources are likely to influence the use of specific coping strategies.

Looking at our empirical data on coping strategies of Holocaust survivors and immigrants living in the U.S. and in Israel, an interesting pattern was discerned in both countries. Survivors were found to be more likely than immigrants to engage in avoidant and emotional coping. On problem solving orientations to coping, there were generally no significant differences between survivors and immigrants.

We have reported data on coping strategies among Holocaust survivors in our prior work (Kahana, et al., 1988). Coping strategies are activated only in the presence of stressful or problem situations and their utility is likely to depend on the particular problem confronted. Both environmental constraints and opportunities may thus be expected to have impact on modes of coping with stress. It is for these reasons that we do not define absence or presence of given coping strategies as reflections of personal vulnerability in our conceptualization of coping with extreme stress. We argue that processes of coping must be distinguished from both coping resources and the outcomes of coping. Furthermore, different types of coping strategies may be useful in different problem situations (Kahana & Kahana, 1983). Accordingly, instrumental coping may be useful in dealing with stresses of relocation whereas avoidant coping may play a useful buffering role in illness situations. The ability to utilize a spectrum of coping strategies appropriate to the stressors confronted, may be seen as enhancing their effectiveness as buffers in dealing with stressful life situations.

It is important to note that social status characteristics, such as education and income, are generally seen as the resources which help an individual at times of stress and need. Holocaust survivors lost all economic resources and experienced disrupted education. Education and economic resources had to be attained through difficult struggles in new homelands. They comprised postwar achievements whereby survivors could attach themselves to society. Disrupted educational background, and/or lack of knowledge of the language in a new land had to be overcome through coping skills, which enabled survivors to lead useful and productive lives (Krell & Dasberg, 2001).

SEQUELAE OF TRAUMA SURVIVORSHIP

In considering well-being in the aftermath of having endured extreme trauma, we focus on traditional indicators of physical and mental health outcomes. We seek to understand whether survivors and immigrants experienced different types and levels of physical and psychological symptomatology in late life. We thus consider the magnitude as well as the types of problems exhibited by our research participants in each group. In addition to traditional physical and mental health indicators of posttraumatic adjustment, we also consider social functioning and achievements of our research participants.

In the field of traumatic stress research there has been a focus on posttraumatic stress disorder (PTSD) as a manifestation of adverse effects of trauma (McCann, & Pearlman, 1990; Wilson, Friedman, & Lindy, 2001). The view that all who endure inhumanity suffer lasting post-traumatic pathology can lead to the stigmatizing of survivors. As the field of traumatology has progressed, we have increasingly moved from acknowledging ill effects of trauma to also seeking an understanding of healing in its aftermath. A number of recent volumes in the field of traumatic stress reflect this emergent interest and trend. They range from Rothstein's *The Reconstruction of Trauma* (1986), and Wilson's *Trauma, Transformation, and Healing* (1989) to Tedeschi and Calhoun's *Trauma and Transformation* (1995).

A close perusal of these volumes reflects an orientation to look past the trauma, to end the "conspiracy of silence", to stop blaming the victims and to understand coping skills of survivors. Yet, a disproportionate share of empirical research in this field is still focused only on the ill effects of trauma on victims, relatively few studies offer data relevant to healing and transcendence of trauma (Shmotkin & Lomranz, 1998). Perhaps, a major need in achieving a better understanding of healing is the introduction of conceptual frameworks for understanding recovery. Our goal of the present study has been to incorporate a focus on healing and recovery (Tedeschi & Calhoun, 1995). Thus we consider how survivors have been able to build new lives in the aftermath of great stressors endured. The concept of coping can be usefully invoked as a moderator in the framework of the stress paradigm as we consider positive achievements of trauma survivors.

We also move beyond examining performance on traditional coping inventories to seeking understanding of more macro levels of behavioral coping. Our study of survivors can thus be integrated with our work on models of successful aging which focus on proactive adaptation or behavioral coping as a cornerstone of maintaining high quality of life in the face of normative stressors of aging (Kahana & Kahana, 1996; 2003). For survivors who relocated either to the U.S. or to Israel, acculturation was a necessary behavioral adaptation to insure integration in a new social environment. Survivors needed to build social supports in order to reduce their isolation, and to overcome the stigma of having endured the Holocaust. Immersion in work helped survivors ward off intrusive memories of trauma and also contributed to building both economic resources and social networks in the aftermath of their wartime experiences. Building a close family of procreation after the loss of their family of origin during the Holocaust was also of great importance. The ability to establish close families of procreation helped survivors surround themselves with people they could trust and helped build social supports prior to reaching old age.

In terms of behavioral adaptations, self-disclosure can play an important role in diminishing psychological isolation of Holocaust survivors (Hemenover, 2003). Self-disclosures can also pave the way for marshalling support for times when older adults have to face normative stressors of aging (Kahana & Kahana, 2003; Pennebaker, 1995). Discussions about the Holocaust would help survivors move from negative self-concepts of having been a helpless victim, to far more positive self-concepts of the active storyteller (Wolfenstein, 1957). Social integration with fellow survivors could also prove to be helpful as elderly survivors experience new normative social losses, especially through widowhood or death of close friends or family (Kahana & Kahana, 2003; Pennebaker, 1995).

FACING OLD AGE IN THE AFTERMATH OF THE HOLOCAUST

Research indicates that people who did not show psychological symptomatology earlier may start to be symptomatic in old age (Landau & Litwin, 2000). The "vulnerability" perspective argues that the experience of trauma earlier in the life span may leave people vulnerable and less able to cope with other negative life events. Moreover, old age is a time when people experience losses associated with aging (death of spouse, relocation of friends, physical decline etc.) (Kahana & Kahana, 1996). Therefore, old age may be conceptualized as a period of life when survivors become vulnerable to "reexperiencing" previous psychological trauma. For example, retirement, which can represent loss of an important social role may leave elderly survivors with free time to reminisce about their past life (Bar-Tur & Levy-Shiff, 2000). Old age is also a time when people return to memories and attempt to integrate them with their current life and with evaluation of their life course (Butler, 2002). For Holocaust survivors, such reminiscence about the past may "rekindle" the old traumatic memories, leaving them depressed and grieving for their losses. These reactions may be diagnosed as depression in old age among the survivors (Danieli, 1997).

Moreover, it has been argued that old age may actually work as a trigger for PTSD symptoms or act to exacerbate them (Port, Engdahl, Frazier, & Eberly, 2002). Normative negative life events in old age, such as the loss of spouse and friends may act as reminders of non-normative earlier losses associated with the Holocaust (Cohen, Dekel, & Solomon, 2002). Physical decline and illness may evoke feelings of vulnerability since being sick and frail meant "death" at work camps during the Holocaust (Arendt, 1964).

The 'inoculation perspective' as opposed to the 'vulnerability perspective' argues that aging Holocaust survivors do not necessarily experience special adverse reactions in old age. On the contrary, survivors may feel strengthened in old age. They may feel that surviving into old age is a triumph permitting them to contribute to the maintenance of the culture of a people that was intended to be annihilated. Therefore, reminiscence in old age does not necessarily bring back old traumatic memories. Rather, it may contribute to the joyful feeling of being alive in old age, surrounded by grandchildren and other loved ones. Accordingly, Shmotkin, Blumstein, and Modan (2003) argue that the ultimate test of the long-term effects of the Holocaust on survivors would be a longitudinal study tracing the psychosocial changes taking place in the lives of the survivors in as they age.

Researchers also acknowledge the importance of the existence of psychosocial protective resources in enabling the survivors to rebuild their lives. Strong marital bonds and having a successful career could enable survivors to focus on the present and future. Moreover, one must consider complex interactions between prewar experiences, personality, and the nature of the traumatic experience. The worst psychological outcomes are reported to be associated with having lived in concentration camps as opposed to being in hiding or in labor camps (Lev-Wiesel, 2000). Furthermore, post-Holocaust life events also contribute to a dynamic multifactorial model determining late life outcomes for survivors (Bar-Tur & Levy-Shiff, 2000).

Another interpretation of late life experiences of Holocaust survivors poses a dual focus on vulnerability and inoculation perspectives. It is argued that even though the majority of the survivors are socially and occupationally well functioning, there may be deep-buried, unresolved issues that may become more obvious in times of crisis. Sadovoy (1997) argues that "emotional reactivity may remain intense and dysphoric without affecting measures of adaptation and overt behavior" (p. 290.). Such response to new trauma was found among Holocaust survivors who showed more symptoms of stress during the Gulf War compared to a control sample (Shmotkin et al., 2003). Holocaust survivors with cancer are also reported to have higher levels of distress as compared to cancer patients who had not gone through the Holocaust (Levan, 1998). Such findings suggest that, even though Holocaust survivors adapted to the instrumental aspects of life, and function well socially, they still carry "psychological scars" which are reopened by new trauma (Shmotkin et al., 2003).

Data from the present study support the value of going beyond evaluating central tendencies or averages in evaluating well-being of Holocaust survivors, and consider their adaptation as reflecting typologies of response. Thus, for example, consideration of adaptation to aging in our sample of survivors based on qualitative responses by survivors was found to fall into four distinct categories (Seckin, Kahana, Kahana, & King, 2002). Respondents replied to open-ended questions, evaluating their own aging and comparing them to others who did not endure the trauma of the Holocaust.

Typologies include "Resilient Agers", "Conditionally Vulnerable Agers", Premature Agers", and "Parallel Agers". Resilient agers express a positive self-concept focusing on sources of strength and a strong sense of values in the face of adversity. Conditionally vulnerable agers express a sense of healing from adverse sequelae of the Holocaust with the elapsing of time. However, their wounds are readily re-opened as they confront new losses or stressors during later life. Premature agers are older individuals who express enduring distress in the aftermath of trauma. They focus on the overwhelming nature of these negative outcomes. These respondents often express beliefs that their traumatic experiences may have precipitated premature aging. Parallel agers focus on the comparability of their aging to others who did not endure trauma. They view aging as an equalizer, which metes out normative stressors to all individuals who survive later life.

Furthermore, even when elderly Holocaust survivors show special symptoms of distress, symptomatology may be viewed as normal human psychological reaction to an abnormal situation. Interpretation of research results regarding the psychological well-being and mental health of Holocaust survivors must be approached with the realization that survivors endured horrific experiences where they were forced to live in and respond to a prolonged abnormal situation (Shmotkin & Lomranz, 1998). Resolving and coming to terms with a trauma which involved efforts aimed to exterminate a whole culture and its people is a daunting task (Sagi-Schwartz, Van Ijzendoorn, Grosmman, Joels, Grosmman, Scharf, Koren-Karin, & Alkalay, 2003).

For elderly Holocaust survivors, outcomes of success can also move from personal and social criteria of success to elements of what Tornstam (1992) terms "gerotranscendance." Accordingly, in considering elderly Holocaust survivors, our discussions must move from consequences of suffering to consequences of survivorship. Reflections of long-term survivors on the meaning of their lives suggest a sense of responsibility for both personal and community survival.

In this chapter, we laid the conceptual groundwork for considering late life adaptations of Holocaust survivors. In the next chapter we focus in greater depth on the lived experience of Holocaust survivors during the war years. A glimpse of their experiences recounted in their own words will set the stage for quantitative results about late life sequlae of trauma presented in the following chapters.

REFERENCES

Amir, M., & Lev-Wiesel, R. (2003). Quality of life and psychological distress of people who survived the Holocaust as children 55 years later, *Journal of Traumatic Stress*, 16(3): 295–299.

Antonucci, T. C. (1991). Attachment, Social Support, and Coping with Negative Life Events in Mature Adulthood. In E. M. Cummings & A.L. Greene (Eds). *Life Span Developmental Psychology: Perspectives on Stress and Coping*: 261–276. Hillsdale, N.J.: L. Erlbaum Associates.

Antonovsky, A. (1979). *Health, Stress, and Coping*. San Francisco: Jossey-Bass.

Atchley, R.C. & Baruch, A. (2004). *Social Forces and Aging*. Belmont, CA: Wadsworth/Thomson Learning, 2004.

Bar-Tur, L. & Levy-Shiff, R. (2000). Coping with losses and past trauma in old age: The separation-individuation perspective, *Psychology and Behavioral Sciences Collection*, 5(2/3): 263–282.

Bauer, Y. & Rotenstreich, N. (1981). *The Holocaust as Historical Experience: Essays and a discussion*. New York: Holmes and Meier.

Billings, A.G., & Moos, H. (1982). Stressful life events and symptoms: A longitudinal model, *Health Psychology*, 1(2): 99–117.

Butler, R.N. (2002). The Life Review, *Journal of Geriatric Psychiatry*, 35(1): 7–10.

Caplan, G. (1989). Recent developments in crisis intervention and the promotion of support service, *Journal of Primary Prevention*, 10(1): 3–25.

Chaitin, J. (2003). Living with the past. Coping and patterns in families of Holocaust survivors, *Family Process*, 42(2): 305–322.

Cobb, S. (1976). Social Support as a moderator of life stress. *Psychosomatic Medicine*, 38(5): 300–314.

Cohen, E., Dekel, R., & Solomon, Z. (2002). Long-term adjustment and the role of attachment among Holocaust child survivors, *Personality and Individual Differences*, 33: 299–310.

Danieli, Y. (1997). As survivors age: An overview. *Journal of Geriatric Psychiatry*, 30(1), 9–26.

Dohrenwend, B. S. & Dohrenwend, B. P. (1984). Life Stress and Illness: Formulation of the Issues. In B. S. Dohrenwend & B. P. Dohrenwend (Eds.), *Stressful Life Events and Their Contexts*, (pp. 1–27). New Brunswick, NJ: Rutgers University Press.

George, L. (1990). "Vulnerability and Social Factors". In Z. Harel, P. Ehrlich, & R. Hubbard (Eds.): *Vulnerable Aged: People, Policies, and Programs*. New York: Springer.

George, L., Siegler, I.C. (1981). *Coping with Stress and Coping in Later Life: Older People Speak for Themselves*. Durham, NC: Center for the Study of Aging and Human Development and Department of Psychiatry, Duke University Medical Center.

Goulet, L.R., & Baltes, P.B. (Eds.)(1970). *Life-Span Developmental Psychology: Research and Theory*. New York: Academic Press.

Harel, Z. (Ed.), Ehrlich, P. (Ed.), & Hubbard, R. W (Ed.). (1990). *The Vulnerable Aged. People, Services, and Policies*. New York, NY: Springer Publishing Co.

Hemenover, S.H. (2003). The good, the bad, and the healthy: Impacts of emotional disclosure of trauma on resilient self-concept and psychological distress, *Personality and Social Psychology Bulletin*, 29(10): 1236–1244.

Hilberg, R. (1985). The *Destruction of European Jews*. New York: Holmes & Meier.

Kahana, B., & Kahana, E. (1983). Stress reactions. In P. Lewinsohn, & L. Teri (Eds.), *Clinical Geropsychology*, (pp. 139–169). New York, NY: Pergamon Press.

Kahana, E., Midlarsky, E., & Kahana, B. (1987). Beyond dependency, autonomy, and exchange: Prosocial behavior in late-life adaptation, *Social Justice Research*, 1 (4), 439–459.

Kahana, E., Kahana, B., & Young, R. (1987). Strategies of coping and post institutional outcomes, *Research on Aging*, 9(2): 182–189.

Kahana, E., Kahana, B., & Kinney, J. (1990). Coping among vulnerable elders. In Z. Harel, P. Ehrlich, & R. Hubbard (Eds.). *The Vulnerable Aged: People, Services, and Policies* (pp. 64–85). New York, NY: Springer Publishing Co.

Kahana, E. (1992). Stress Research, and Aging: Complexities, Ambiguities, Paradoxes, and Promise. In M. Wykle, E. Kahana, & J. Kowal (Eds.). *Stress and Health Among the Elderly* (pp. 239–256). New York, NY: Springer Publishing Company.

Kahana, E., & Kahana, B. (1996). Conceptual and Empirical Advances in Understanding Aging Well Through Proactive Adaptation. In V. Bengtson (Ed.). *Adulthood and Aging: Research on Continuities and Discontinuities* (pp. 18–40). New York, NY: Springer Publishing Co.

Kahana, B., & Kahana, E. (1998). Toward a Temporal-Spatial Model of Cumulative Life Stress: Placing Late Life Stress Effects in Life Course Perspective. In J. Lomranz, (Ed.), *Handbook of Aging and Mental Health: An Integrative Approach.* (pp.153–178). New York, NY: Plenum Publishing Co.

Kahana, E., & Kahana, B. (2003). Contextualizing Successful Aging: New Directions in Age-Old Search. In R. Settersten, Jr. (Ed.). *Invitation to the Life Course: A New Look at Old Age.* (pp. 225–255). Amityville, NY: Baywood Publishing Company.

Kahana, E., Kahana, B., Harel, Z., & Rosner, T. (1988). Coping with extreme trauma. In J. Wilson, Z. Harel, & B. Kahana (Eds.), *Human Adaptation to Extreme Stress: From the Holocaust to Vietnam* (pp. 55–79). New York: Plenum.

Kellerman, N.F. (2001). The long-term psychological effects and treatment of Holocaust trauma, *Journal of Loss and Trauma*, 6: 197–218.

Krause, N. (1991). Stressful events and life satisfaction among elderly men and women. *Journals of Gerontology*, 46 (2), S84–S92.

Krell, R., & Dasberg, H. (2001). *Messages and Memories: Reflections on Child Survivors of Holocaust.* Vancouver, B.C: Memory Press.

Krell, R. (2001). The Challenges of Being a Child Survivor of the Holocaust. In R. Krell, H. Dasberg (Eds.). *Messages and Memories: Reflections on Child Survivors of Holocaust.* (pp. 95–106). Vancouver, B.C: Memory Press.

Landau, R., & Litwin, H. (2000). The effects of extreme early stress in very old age, *Journal of Traumatic Stress*, 13(3): 473–487.

Lawton, M.P. (1983). Environment and other determinants of well-being in older people. *Gerontologist*, 23(4): 349–357.

Lazarus, R.S. & Folkman, S. (1984). *Stress, Appraisal, and Coping.* New York: Springer.

Lev-Wiesel, R. (2000). Posttraumatic stress disorder symptoms, psychological distress, personal resources, and quality of life in four groups of holocaust survivors. *Family Process*, 39(4): 445–459.

Maddox, G. (Ed.) (2001). *The Encyclopedia of Aging. A Comprehensive Resource in Gerontology and Geriatrics.* New York: Springer Publishing.

McCann, L. & Pearlman, L. (1990). *Psychological Trauma and the Adult Survivor.* New York: Brunner/Mazel.

McCrae, R.R., & Costa, P.T. (1986). Personality, coping, and coping effectiveness, in an adult sample, *Journal of Personality*, 54(2): 385–405.

McGrath, J.E. (1970). *Social and Psychological Factors in Stress.* Oxford, England: Holt, Rinehart & Winston.

Moskovitz, S. (2001). Making Sense of Survival. In R. Krell & H. Dasberg (Eds.). *Messages and Memories: Reflections on Childhood Survivors of the Holocaust.* (pp.11–26). Vancouver, B.C: Memory Press:

Pearlin, L.I. & Schooler, C. (1978). The structure of coping. *Journal of Health & Social Behavior*, 19(1), 2–21.

Pearlin, L.I., Menaghan, E.G., Lieberman, M.A., & Mullan, J.T. (1981). The stress process. *Journal of Health & Social Behavior*, 22(4), 337–356.

Pearlin, L.I. (1989). The sociological study of stress. *Journal of Health & Social Behavior*, 30(3), 241–256.

Pennebaker, J.W. (1995). *Emotion, Disclosure, & Health.* Washington, DC: American Psychological Association.

Port, C.L., Engdahl, B., Frazier, P., & Eberly, R. (2002). Factors related to the long term course of PTSD in older ex-prisoners of war. *Journal of Clinical Geropsychology*, 8(3): 203–214.

Raphael, B. (1986). When *Disaster strikes: How Individuals and Communities Cope with Catastrophe.* New York: Basic Books.

Rosow, J. (1967). *Social Integration of the Aged.* New York: The Free Press.

Rothstein, A. (Ed.). (1986). *The Reconstruction of Trauma. Its Significance in Clinical Work.* Madison, CT: International University Press, Inc.

Sadavoy, J. (1997). A review of the late-life effects of prior psychological trauma, *The American Journal of Geriatric Psychiatry*, 5(4): 287–301.

Sagi-Schwartz, A., van Ijzendoorn, M.H., Grossman, K.E., Joels, T., Grossman, K., Scharf, M., Koren-Karie, N., & Alkalay, S. (2003). Attachment and traumatic stress in female

Holocaust child survivors and their daughters, *The American Journal of Psychiatry*, 160: 1086–1092.

Seckin, G., Kahana, E. Kahana, B., *King, C. (2002). *Typology of traumatized elderly as applied to alternative sources of trauma*. Paper presented at the 55th Annual Conference of the Gerontological Society of America, Boston MA.

Shmotkin, D., & Lomranz, J. (1998). Subjective well-being among Holocaust survivors. An examination of overlooked differentiations, *Journal of Personality and Social Psychology*, 75(1): 141–155.

Shmotkin, D., Blumstein, T., & Modan, B. (2003). Tracing long-term effects of early trauma. A broad scope view of Holocaust survivors in late life, *Journal of Consulting and Clinical Psychology*, 71(2): 223–234.

Sigal, J.J. (1998). Long-term effects of the Holocaust: Empirical evidence for resilience in the first, second, and third generation, *Psychoanalytic Review*, 85(4): 579–585.

Stephens, M.P., Norris, V.K., Kinney, J.M., Ritchie, S.W., & Grotz, R.C. (1988). Stressful situations in care giving: Relations between caregiver coping and well-being. *Psychology & Aging*, 3(2), 208–209.

Tanay, E. (2004). *Passport to Life: Autobiographic Reflections on the Holocaust*. Ann Arbor, Michigan: Forensic.

Tedeschi, R.G. & Calhoun, L.G. (1995). *Trauma and Transformation: Growing in the Aftermath of Suffering*. Thousand Oaks, CA: Sage Publications.

Tornstam, L. (1992). The quo vadis of gerontology: On the scientific paradigm of gerontology. *The Gerontologist*, 32(3), 318–326.

Wheaton, B. (1997). The Nature of Chronic Stress. In B.H. Gottlieb (ed.). *Coping with Chronic Stress*. New York: Plenum press.

Wilson, J.P. (1989). *Trauma, Transformation, and Healing: an Integrative Approach to Theory, Research, and Post-Traumatic Therapy*. New York: Brunner/Mazel.

Wilson, J.P., Friedman, M.J., & Lindy, J.D. (2001). *Treating Psychological Trauma and PTSD*. New York: The Guilford Press.

Wolfenstein, M. (1957). *Disaster. A Psychological Essay*. Illinois: Free Press.

2

The Holocaust Years
Survivors Share Their Wartime Experiences

INTRODUCTION

Before presenting data on our quantitative study of the functioning and well-being of Holocaust survivors in the aftermath of the trauma they endured, it is useful to provide a glimpse into the phenomenology of survivors as they recount their traumatic experiences. We also need to outline the historical reality that defined the man-made disaster known as the Holocaust. This chapter provides information from responses to qualitative questions by Jewish survivors of the Holocaust. They experienced the war in diverse countries of Europe including Germany, Austria, France, Holland, Belgium, Poland, Ukraine, Czechoslovakia, Hungary and Romania. The interviews provide glimpses of the stresses and coping responses of persons who were prisoners in concentration camps, part of the resistance movement or were refugees in hiding. The chapter is organized into sections: first we offer a general background detailing critical dates of anti-Semitic policies as these were implemented in the various countries. Then the focus shifts to a review of first-hand accounts of the stresses endured in the different countries where the respondents weathered the Holocaust.

The perpetration of the atrocities of the Holocaust may be seen as a collective endeavor in the Europe of those days. The leadership for the oppression and extermination of the Jews was masterminded and championed by Hitler and his administration (Hilberg, 1985; Bauer & Rotenstreich, 1981). Willing European countries cooperated in carrying out Hitler's master plan. The Fascist regimes and political parties in various countries helped in rounding up and killing Jews. There were, however, notable exceptions to this general trend. Sweden and Great Britain were willing to admit Jewish persons who managed to escape from Germany and German occupied countries. Denmark saved ninety five percent of its Jewry. Italy saved close to seventy percent of its Jewish population. Throughout other European countries there were also rescuers, "righteous gentiles" who risked their own lives to hide, aid and save Jews (Hillberg, 1992).

This chapter focuses on the stresses Jewish victims endured as the Nazis came into power, their experiences under Nazi occupation, life in hiding and in the concentration camps. Survivors share their responses about the way they coped when they were exposed to brutal sights, sounds, and experiences. They share some of the usual and unusual ways of coping and portray how individual situations varied. Respondents provide glimpses of the concentration camps, the ways these differed from one another, and how their organization impacted upon the lives of the prisoners. The survivors' answers to open ended questions, as they tell their lived experience, enhance our knowledge and understanding of the ways that Holocaust survivors endured and coped with their traumatic experiences and losses during the World War II years.

HISTORICAL BACKGROUND

On January 30, 1939, Hitler delivered a speech to the Reichstag prophesizing that war would bring the "annihilation of the Jewish race in Europe'" (Arendt, 1964). By September 1939, the necessary bureaucratic structures were established to begin the fulfillment of this master plan for which Hitler easily found able and willing helpers (Goldhagen, 1996). And, by 1945, a total of 12 million people, including 6 million innocent Jews had been exterminated. What took place between the years of 1939, when the Nazi regime became "openly totalitarian and openly criminal," and 1945, when the defeat of Nazi Germany had become an inevitable reality, is simply beyond human comprehension and understanding. How the most enlightened nation of those days could impose on innocent people torture, physical and mental torment and barbaric death defies rational answers. For what began in the eyes of many (both Jews and non-Jews) as arrests and deportation policies leading to "resettlement," in reality were the seeds leading to a unified policy of extermination. Hitler was outspokenly anti-Semitic. He made it quite clear that he saw the Jews as the cause of all Germany's economic and social problems (Yahil, 1990). This open anti-Semitism actually worked to his advantage, for other European countries had severe economic problems resulting from the post World War One, depression and they too were vulnerable to propaganda, which offered them a scapegoat. In addition, tensions were aggravated by the fact that in some countries the number of foreign Jews (mostly from Germany) had dramatically increased during the pre-World War II years (many Jews had fled their native countries to escape persecution), while in other countries many Jews had never fully been assimilated into native culture (Arendt, 1964; Yahil, 1990). Yahil (1990) writes:

"The world's sovereign states were just then beginning to recover from the most severe economic crisis the world had known for decades. Historically, the masses of Jews had always been the first to suffer from any kind of crisis in their host countries: politically, economically, socially and/or spiritually. In the 1930's all four such crises were combined: the spiritual crisis opened the floodgates of anti-Semitism; the economic and social crises led to the closing of borders to immigration; and the political crisis gave rise to the policy of appeasement, which forestalled effective political action on behalf of the persecuted Jews in Germany, Austria, and Czechoslovakia" (Yahil, 1990, pp. 90–91).

In those European countries, large segments of the Jewish populations were regarded as undesirable. Hitler was able to capitalize on these nationalistic tendencies and propose a "solution" to the "Jewish problem." Hitler's goal was to make Germany (and later all of his occupied countries) "Judenrein", or free of the Jews, as quickly as possible.

In March 1939 when Hitler invaded Czechoslovakia, an emigration center was established at the capital city of Prague. This set the tone for other nations to follow. Explicit German arrangements and rationalization helped to create the illusion that it was perfectly normal for countries to be "Judenrein" and to deport their Jews. Hundreds of thousands of Jews left on their own where they could. Others were forced to leave their homelands in a matter of a few years. Governments that allied themselves with Germany left no doubt in their official proclamations that they, too, wished to be rid of their Jews. They could not understand why the world should get indignant if they followed in the footsteps of Germany "a great and cultured nation" (Arendt, 1964).

In 1939, as the war began, Germany invaded Poland where two and a half million Jews lived. Forced evacuations of Jews was started eastward towards the occupied German territory in Poland. By December 1939, one million Jews (six hundred thousand Jews from the occupied Polish territory and 400,000 from the Reich) were deported to the occupied areas in Poland, leaving behind all their possessions, except the belongings which they could carry with them (Arendt, 1964). At that time it became obvious to the Germans that emigration was not an efficient way of making the Reich Judenrein (free of Jews). Not only was the process a bureaucratic fiasco, but they also realized that there was no territory, which could accommodate the nearly seven million Jews of Europe. Violence against the Jews became commonplace, though a unified policy of extermination did not officially begin until the Germans invaded Russia in June 1941 (Hilberg, 1985).

According to Adolf Eichmann, one of the men first involved in the emigration of the Jews and later implicated as a chief figure in the extermination programs, the invasion of Russia symbolized "the end of an era in which there existed laws, ordinances, and decrees for the treatment of the Jews" (Eichmann, as quoted by Arendt, 1964:78). Auschwitz, the largest of all the concentration camps built during the war, was established during the spring of 1940. At first, only Poles and Jews were interned there. Then in June 1941, Czechs and Jews from other countries began to arrive in the camp. Soviet soldiers captured in the invasion were sent to extermination camps, where they were killed immediately. After the Russian killings, the mass murder of Jews began, based on a policy of racial inferiority. In September 1941, Zyklon B gas was used for the first time, and by January 1942 at Auschwitz, Jews were being routinely sent to the gas chambers. The extermination program employed two dominant methods of killing: by gas and by shooting. Before the crematoria were built in the concentration camps, mobile gas vans were used. The following is a description of what Eichmann witnessed at Chelmno, a concentration camp located in Poland:

> "The Jews were in a large room; they were told to strip; then a truck arrived, stopping directly before the entrance to the room, and the naked Jews were told to enter it. The doors were closed and the truck started off. I cannot tell how many Jews entered, I hardly looked. I could not; I could not; I had had enough. I was much too upset, and so on, as I later told Muller when I reported to him; he did not get much profit from my report. I then drove along after the van, and then I saw the most horrible sight I had thus far seen in my life. The truck was making for an open ditch, the doors were opened, and the corpses were thrown out, as though they were still alive, so smooth were their limbs. They were hurled into the ditch, and I can still see a civilian extracting the teeth with tooth pliers. And then I was off—jumped into my car and did not open my mouth any more. After that time, I could sit for hours beside my driver without exchanging a word with him. There I got enough. I was finished. I only remember that a physician in white overalls told me to look through a hole into the truck while they were still in it. I refused to do that. I could not. I had to disappear." (Eichmann, in Arendt, 1964:88).

In January 1942, the Wannsee Conference was convened and issued the directive that the Final Solution (or extermination) should be applied to all European Jews. The plan was to be implemented in stages. First, Jews were to be isolated from the native populations (by being forced to wear a yellow badge and put into ghettos) and then declared stateless. Thus, no country could inquire about their fate, and the fascist governments could take their property (Arendt, 1964). Anti-Jewish action always started with stateless persons.

Against the context of the unspeakable horrors documented by historians, survivor accounts reviewed in this chapter represent firsthand testimonies of their experiences as the final solution was carried out in their respective countries. As may be seen in these pages, the stages of the final solution were replicated methodically the same way in various European countries. First came the terror associated with the Nazi invasion, then the imposition of oppression and practices of discrimination, followed by displacement from home and confiscation of possessions and internment in the ghetto, and, finally, deportations to work or death camps. For some, these events resulted in their escape into hiding and for some others in joining resistance units.

GERMAN INVASION OF POLAND IN 1939

Poland was the country that was most vulnerable to Hitler's policies. Hitler's goal was not only to make Poland "Judenrein", but also to reduce the Polish people to a nation of second-class citizens. Educated persons in Poland, intellectuals, landowners, and professionals were to be taken to annihilation camps. Those remaining were to serve as slaves to their German "masters" (Yahil, 1990).

The infiltration of evil into the lives of both Poles and Polish Jews started immediately after Nazis invaded Poland. Jews in particular became the first victims of the Nazi terror. As one respondent notes: "There was no question of satisfying the Nazis-just by being a Jew they were after you." The Jewish star was introduced in Poland in 1939, one of the first steps in the process of systematic genocide. It was not introduced into the German Reich until 1941 (Arendt, 1964). Homes were taken away from their owners, property was confiscated, and families were separated. Men and children in particular could be kidnapped and taken away at any time by the Nazis to work in their labor camps or to be killed. Jews were threatened with death if there was any resistance. In the following interview, one of the respondents in our study describes the treatment he and his family endured as Hitler's army entered his city.

"We had to leave home when the Germans came in, September 1, 1939. At five a.m. Hitler attacked Poland and when the Nazis came into our city they took us out of our house, my whole family, and they took us in a place and put us on a line with other Jews, 60 or 70 people, and they had a machine gun and pointed it at all of us and told us to wait there. Then a German soldier came out from the building and he told us he would let us free if we tell everybody in the city "if one German got killed, they'll kill all the Jews." So we went home and he let us go free."

The above incident provides a glimpse of the way the Nazis wielded their power. They treated innocent people like criminals, using weapons (in this case machine guns) to underscore their authority. Jews were the Nazi scapegoats, as may be seen in various personal testimonies, the threats made to them by the Nazis were in no way idle; Jews were to subjugate themselves to al Nazi demands or else, be killed.

From the value of obedience, the imperative to obey Nazi authority blindly was derived. Out of the recognition of strength as a value came the imperative to apply strength with brutality. Recognition of national and racial superiority entailed the subsequent actions to enslave and exterminate "inferior" races and nations. The uncertainty and precariousness of Jewish life as the Nazis entered Poland in 1939 may be seen in the account of another survivor who lived in Lubaczow (a Polish border town) in 1939:

> "The Nazis came in for a short time (several months). Then they made an agreement with the Russians who came to our town and were there until 1941. We knew what was going on in Germany but they were not there long enough. We were scared-did not know what was going to happen.... There were general problems that faced all the Jews such as Hitler, listening to his speeches, reading the papers, and worrying what [will] lie ahead for us".

Another respondent describes how the Nazi invasion was particularly obtrusive and destructive in Warsaw, the capital city of Poland, where he was living in 1939. In addition to trying to physically survive in a city under siege, Jews in Warsaw faced a more ominous problem, their rights as citizens were revoked.

> "They [the Nazis] marched in September 28, 1939. Life became very intolerable. We couldn't walk down the street. They grabbed Jews from the street for work and you never knew if you were going to come home or not. They kept us from morning to late at night doing hard work for nothing. They'd beat [us].... When the war began we had no food. They bombed the first day. The only places we could go were to the bombed places. Pickles, sardines, that's what we brought home to eat. The bombing was going on. We had no electricity or water".

> "It was very tough. The bombs started dropping on my city where I was born. Ninety percent of everything was bombed and they made the ghetto. They beat us and made us work hard. Some of my friends, they [the Nazis] cut their hair. I got in the ghetto and saw that it was bad and they work me to death...."

All across Poland as the Nazi seizure of power became more secure, every effort was made to destroy Jewish businesses and family life. Fear began to replace uncertainty as the Nazi brutality became more systematic. Two respondents relate their experiences:

> "We were fearful to walk out of the house, fearful when they would come and kill us because that's what they started doing right away. If they saw young kids in the streets they got them together and sent them away to other places and parents didn't know where the kids were."

> "I was still working; books were very saleable at that time. I worked there [in a printing shop] for a while. All of a sudden they started to close up the printing shops. One day when I was alone there, they came to see what I was printing and started to beat me up. Then they threw me out and sealed the shop. The owner of the shop was shot in the street. Me, they let go. They beat me up and let me go. They torched the machines."

Another survivor provides a particularly poignant description of the fear experienced by a family being hunted by the Nazis. In describing her own family situation, she exposes the abuses imposed particularly upon the male members of Jewish families who were the first targets of Nazi brutality and savagery:

> "The family was scattered, emotionally broken. When Germans came in we were afraid. My father had to hide. He hid in a room and we covered the door with a dresser. My mother stayed in the store and my father stayed hidden in a room in the house for two weeks until the Germans left-they were looking for all men, mainly just to degrade them, cutting their beards off and making them do degrading jobs. Everybody tried to live a normal life but everybody was afraid. But after six months they put my father in jail in 1940, because of political reason. Never saw him again. He was put in jail in our town and then sent to jail in Kiev, then I understand when the Germans came into Kiev the Germans killed them."

Separation policies were introduced in November, 1939, and these policies were symbolically represented by the yellow Jewish star which all Jews were required to wear at all times (Arendt, 1964). One survivor describes what she felt about being segregated from others and experiencing the implementation of discriminatory policies: food rationing, restriction of movement, and finally randomized killing:

> "We were treated like animals not like humans; distressful. We couldn't walk on the sidewalks, we had to walk in the streets and wear yellow arm bands with the Star of David on it".

> "You saw right away they started to ration the food. You couldn't buy what you wanted and you couldn't walk where you wanted. They started to kill right away a lot of people and there wasn't any reason for it."

Anxiety was exacerbated by the fact that the Jews, experiencing restrictions in all spheres of life, could do little to combat the situation. In the views of the Nazis and their collaborators they had no rights. Another stress as the war began in 1939 was the antipathy between the Poles and the Jews. Both groups were condemned to death, yet their shared fate did little to bring the two groups together. Another survivor notes that the local population often cooperated with the Germans:

> "The Germans, with the help of the local population took the men away to a labor camp and expelled the women and children from the city. The women went to different cities and we found out later that they killed all the men."

The estrangement and lack of cooperation between Poles and Jews may have been exacerbated by the uncertainty and immorality which the Nazi rule encouraged. Individual heroic resistance usually meant death, and fear frequently prevented defensive actions. At the same time, the situation of extreme terror produced in everyone a sense of abandonment and recognition of the futility of defending oneself.

As a result of this general distrust, many Jews felt that they could only rely upon each other for support. Decision-making was often random and emotional, no one knew what to do, especially when families were torn apart (with the men being taken by the Nazis). The following interview reveals the nightmare of being uprooted and hunted by the Germans without being able to get support of friends or a secure plan of action:

> "It was a mess. Everybody was looking for a way to survive. Everyone was running this way and that way, all confused. We were ready to go to Russia but my mother was crying so I decided to stay in our house. My father was gone. He was picked up from the street and I never saw him again. At that time we heard of a place where in a forest there were mass graves and where they undressed them all naked and the machine guns shot them and they fell into the open graves. There was no ghetto yet. We lived on the Jewish street we thought that our street would be made a ghetto. One morning my mother, aunt, little sister, and brother were home with me when we heard in the courtyard screaming. We thought Germans came and took the men but we saw they took women and children, everybody, and there was screaming. I said to my mother, "let's hide someplace" and she said "where"?. I went in the kitchen and I saw a dishtowel and asked my mother to hold the dishtowel while I climbed down to a different court. Then she and the kids and aunt would come after me, so she agreed. I climbed down and sat on a neighbor's windowsill and I called "Mom". She said "they may believe me [that] I am not Jewish. It is too hard to climb down." I was frustrated, scared. Suddenly I heard my mother say "I am no Jew" and the Germans asked for documents. At that time I had to start running-it was pitch dark. I couldn't see anything. Suddenly I realized I was in a steam house and knowing I couldn't go further I lay down, urinated so much I was lying in my own urine and was very scared and shaky-heard screaming-yelling. When I thought all was quiet I got up and started to walk, and the Germans heard my footsteps and I ran back to the same place and lay down again. Somehow they didn't see me with the flashlight and I made sure to lay there awhile. Then I got up and walked back to the house and went upstairs and everybody was gone. The house was like ransacked, everything over the floor. Out of 100 neighbors, five survived. I never saw my mother and family again since that time."

DISPLACEMENT AND GHETTO LIFE

Most of the Polish respondents report that displacement from their homes began around 1940. This would coincide with the evacuation policy, authorized by Himmler on October 30, 1939, which involved the deportation of approximately one million Poles and Polish Jews from Reich territory to the Eastern area of Poland, including Warsaw and Krakow (Yahil, 1990). Displacement from home, friends and possessions may be seen as one of the initial debilitating stresses placed upon Jews and their families (Hilberg, 1985). The following respondent helps to emphasize the impact that displacement had upon her family; they were reduced to a degrading lifestyle:

> "I was very upset that my parents had to leave their home and move to a strange city-leave my friends. We were cooped-up in one room. There were five of us. We were used to a different life and here we had nothing. My father and I went to work."

> "I was expelled from my hometown too, with my mother, a sister and a brother. We went to our grandparents' hometown, which was about sixty miles away. There, they herded us into a ghetto with the rest of the Jewish population."

The second phase of the Nazi terror centered on the ghetto, where many displaced Jews were required to live. Jewish Councils were given administrative power in these ghettos. The ghettos were to serve as general "holding places" for Jews where they could be organized and their property consolidated, before being systematically deported to concentration camps or extermination sites (Gill, 1988). Thus, the ghettos can be seen as the ominous predecessors of the concentration camps.

The conditions in the ghetto were treacherous; poor hygiene in living conditions promoted the spread of disease. There was rarely enough food, and Jews were publicly demeaned and beaten without provocation. In addition, Jews were often made to work long hours for the Germans, without pay. In other words, the ghetto only intensified German anti-Semitic actions and feelings, while undermining Jewish control (Morrison, 2000). Our respondent describes the fear her family felt while living in the ghetto:

> "They took away our business. Our parents were afraid to leave us. We were sent to a smaller town and placed there in a ghetto. My parents wouldn't leave the house because they were beating older people. We had very little food, we were beaten up. Once I sneaked out and tried to get some flour and my mother wanted to make bread and the Gestapo came in and threw the dough on the floor and stamped on it and said "now eat it", and he took all the valuables we had away from us. They caught my father and beat him up and my mother sneaked him in the house and covered him with a mattress and lay on top of it, saying she was sick. They sent their dogs at us and cut half of my father's beard and killed many Jewish persons."

In these interviews we can see the sadism with which the Gestapo exercised their acts of terror. A minor incident, such as leaving the house when unauthorized or during curfew hours, often resulted in severe punishment. The Nazis demanded submission and conformity from the Jews. The slightest deviation from their rules was an excuse for violence or immediate murder. Lodz was the city in Poland with the first organized ghetto (Gill, 1988). One of our respondents describes her experiences in the Lodz ghetto:

> "It was a terrible life. They came in and killed people and took away everything you had in your possession. They made me stop my work and killed my boss and killed almost all the Jewish people. We couldn't go out after 4 pm, we had to stay in the ghetto....

They gave us very little food, we always were hungry . . . It was terrible right away. They pushed us in the ghetto and right away my husband was killed and I was pregnant . . . . We didn't have anything to eat, people were starving. You could not go out in the street or they would kill you. Nothing to describe; we couldn't live and did not die, thousands died of lack of food. The food they gave us, horsemeat from sick horses. I gave birth to a little boy and named him after my husband. He lived just 8 months and died because I had no food for him . . . It was tragic for me to lose my boy but I felt the Nazis would kill him anyway, they killed my sister's kids."

This interview, in particular, reveals the all-encompassing destructive impact of Nazi power on every type of relationship: marital, business, family, and maternal. There were no "special cases", which would allow for example, a pregnant woman to be spared exposure to the devastation. If anything, the pregnant, the elderly, the young children, and the weak received the full impact of Nazi wrath. Another survivor describes his experience of being expelled from his home by the Nazis in 1941 and sent to a newly created ghetto:

"About the 8th or 10th of June, the Nazis came into each household with guns. We felt that things were not going to get better; they took gold, money, and anything valuable. After a few months they created a ghetto and we were told to leave with a few belongings. They took us to the outskirts of the city-the Jewish section-and a man who lived on that section of the town who worked for us, took us in. They also brought in Jews from surrounding sections. It was very crowded, four and five families in a single home. They took us to work each day. We went out every morning to work and then at night we would come home. I worked at a farming job, not too far from where we used to live, a place where we fed the animals and tended to them. We were able to bring in some food and our hope was that someday it will end."

Other families were not as fortunate, as most Jewish families did not have access to food. Those who could not get food had to resort to begging, often from those people who were once neighbors or friends. Our respondents remember their despair and deprivation, often leading to illness and death:

"We went around begging from the Gentile population that used to be friends with our parents. We did get some help from them."

"Not enough to eat. They came every day to send people to death. Had to hide my mother. Always under stress and fear. We ate little, we hungered. Always in fear we'd be transported. Got sick with pneumonia and almost died. My mother got sick and died . . . Everyday was a death sentence."

"We were isolated completely; no radio, no phone, no transportation. If you didn't get a job, you were in constant fear of being taken away. My father died in 1942 from hunger and I could not function because I loved my father."

Throughout these interviews, the lack of food in the ghettos is a pervasive theme, emphasizing its powerful effect on the health and morale of the respondents. The segregation of the Jews in ghettos, their enforced starvation, random beatings, and the exploitation of the Jewish labor force without reimbursement, may be seen as purposeful strategies, which were meant to rob the Jews of their strength and morale, thus weakening their resistance to Nazi power. This could further enable the Nazis to render them as helpless, dependent and portray them as less than human. This made the task physically and emotionally easier to select the weak immediately for death, and later, to transport the rest to concentration camps. Yahil (1990) indicates that these directives served to undermine the foundation of the Jews' lives. This process was built upon a number of basic measures that, taken together, would drain the Jews of their strength to the point where the Nazis could do with them as they pleased.

The first stage entailed the eviction of the Jews from their permanent residences and their deportation to temporary destinations. Second was the concentration and isolation of the Jews, which disrupted their lives, overturned social conventions, and led to insufferable crowding, with all the attendant side effects: dirt, disease, and death. Third, the burden of the organization and maintenance of the deported and concentrated Jews was placed on Jewish communal organizations, administered through the Judenrat. Fourth, confiscating and exploiting their property destroyed the economic basis of Jewish lives. Fifth, the Jewish labor force was exploited. All these measures were but the initial stages of a program that was to lay the ground for achieving "the final solution," which was still considered secret and not yet articulated in clear-cut terms (Yahil, 1990).

Up until 1941, the ghettos were mostly seen as holding places or warehouses for the Jews until the "ultimate solution" could be enacted (Yahil, 1990). However, by 1941, most of the ghettos in Poland were being liquidated, thus becoming the points of transport to the work and death camps, which introduced a new trauma into the lives of ghetto inhabitants. One respondent reflects a feeling of resigned helplessness, as the fate of the Jews became certain:

"There was a ghetto and all the Jews had to go there. From time to time they took some Jews and sent them to the concentration camps.... Every time being in danger of being taken away-they called it "action"...We knew people were being killed, you get used to it, if not today, it will be tomorrow. At that time I had three brothers and two sisters there and my husband and child so we stuck together and suffered together."

The above statement may serve as an example of retrospective memory; the respondent talks as if she knew then, in 1939–40, the fate of the Jews. However, many Jews at that time could not have imagined a fate worse than the ghetto experience. They looked upon their deportation from the ghetto as a release, based on the promise given by the Nazis for a better life. After all, they may have reasoned, they were allowed to take with them their most prized possessions. Their guards told some deportees before being shipped out that they will receive shops and workshops in the new places of settlement and that they will be able to start new lives. However, for many, the horrors of ghetto experience were to pale in comparison with those experiences which they were about to encounter.

CZECHOSLOVAKIA

Using the protection of the Nazis, Slovakia declared its independence from Czechoslovakia on March 14, 1939. One day later, to the welcome of many Slovakians, Hitler entered Czechoslovakia where he was perceived as the liberator (Yahil, 1990; Arendt, 1964). At this time, approximately 90,000 Jews were living in the predominately Catholic state of Czechoslovakia.

Jews in Czechoslovakia were subject to many of the same restrictions, which were being enforced upon the Polish Jews. The only major difference was that in 1939, anti-Jewish measures were based more on religious principles than on political or racist ideology. In addition, at this time, Hitler's attention was not focused primarily on the Czechs, leaving the establishment of anti-Jewish propaganda to the discretion of Slovakia's new leadership. Yahil (1990) writes that a month after the proclamation of the independent state of Slovakia, on April 18, 1939, the new administration published an order imposing restrictions directed at Jewish lawyers. According to the explanation given in the announcement, the concept of a Jew was being defined in order to rectify the social-welfare, economic, and political conditions within Slovakia. As in Germany in 1933, the government of Slovakia was camouflaging its anti-Jewish measures by trying to make their purpose appear to be the welfare of Slovak society as a whole. Following the Nazi example, the rulers of Slovakia proceeded by means of legislation, propaganda, and terror (Yahil, 1990).

Most of our interviews with Holocaust survivors from Czechoslovakia report that the economic, political and social situation of the Jews grew steadily worse from 1939–1942. Survivors attest that beginning in 1939 there was greater animosity against the Jews. Anti-Jewish laws were passed based on the Nuremberg laws and the Nazis ordered the Slovaks to take away Jewish businesses. Little by little they were taking things away from Jews until 1942. Political instability in the region did not improve the deteriorating situation of Jews. The changing national situation increased Jewish fear and uncertainty. The lot of Jews got worse in Slovakia under Hungarian occupation. Our survivors recall those days:

> "In 1942, they took away my parents and sisters and sent them to Auschwitz."

> "The Czechs had to leave that part of the country (the Carpathian area). They left in 1939 and for a short period Ukraine took over and at that time they collaborated with the Nazis. First, I still went to school. The Ukrainaians changed instruction immediately from Czech to the Ukrainian language. I went to school maybe 4 weeks. At that time the Hungarians came in and chased the Ukrainians out. As Jews we already started to feel already some uncertainty. A few weeks later, the Hungarians occupied that part of Slovakia. That was approximately beginning of 1940. I went to the Hungarian school. One day they started up the first hour with the Hungarian prayer and I didn't want to say it so that was my last day of school in the sixth grade. The Hungarians did like what the Germans did to the Jews. They started to take away the Jewish businesses and put their own people in them. They took my father to a labor camp and my mother and seven children were left without any financial support; absolutely nothing. They took away from every Jew their livelihood. We couldn't earn a living."

> "That's when the trouble started. The Hungarians made all sorts of new rules. They took away all the Jewish businesses and gave them to the Gentiles. They made the Jews spend their money to get citizen papers. They took almost everything away, including the fat for cooking."

The general stresses outlined by the Czechoslovakian respondents follow a certain pattern: First there was isolation, discrimination and ridicule. Jews were separated from others on the grounds of their "Jewishness". They experienced exclusion from public places, including sidewalks. Jews were forced to walk in the streets. In 1941, the Jews were forced to wear yellow armbands, which further identified them and thus undermined their status. A frequent comment, which occurred in different forms throughout the interviews, indicated that Jews could not go to certain places and that they could not get jobs because they were Jews. Second came the disregard for their Jewish customs and religion. Third, Jews could not make a living; Jewish businesses were closed and jobs were denied to them. Fourth, Jewish families were broken apart. Males were frequently sent away to forced labor camps, leaving the women and children with no means of supporting themselves. Jews were forced to conform to the orders of the ruling party or risk severe punishment.

Survivor responses underscore these patterns:

> "Everything turned against us. They came out with all kinds of new laws against the Jews; they were not allowed to own property, land, and stores and not allowed to communicate with the non-Jewish population, like friends...Jewish kids could not go on the main street of the town."

> "We had to go to school on the Jewish holiday-that was a big thing."

> "They took everything away from us, the business and the house. They gave us one room to live in and we were afraid of what tomorrow might bring. Only certain times we could

go shopping. You had to have coupons to buy things and nothing was left-we wore yellow armbands marked Jew."

"It was abnormal and they took half the town to be massacred. The difficulties were not knowing where my father was-and we knew Jewish people were up on the front and we had problems with food."

"We were seven children, mother and grandfather without a provider. I had to work very hard which was unusual for a young man like me. I went through very unusual things. I was afraid. I had to travel at night black marketing. I think I became a man before my time. Couldn't continue school or learn a trade. Hungarians made it so much more difficult when they came. It was hard to survive. Situation was very hard. Jews were constantly under pressure. Bread was rationed and sometimes weeks went by they didn't have it. Couldn't go to other area to buy, you would get in trouble with the police."

The implications of these personal reflections were manifold. Jews had no recourse to protection, thus they had no choice but to endure random and often unsolicited beatings. One survivor recalls witnessing the beating of her father and that she too was vulnerable to attack, but of a sexual nature:

"Once they beat up my father so bad-for no reason. My father's brother came from another city and went to the police station. The police beat him up. He came home black and blue. My mother didn't want to let us out."

"The Germans wanted girls. The Nazis came, they went to a restaurant and asked where there were girls and somebody sent them to us. They came to our house and my mother told them we didn't know how to dance. We changed our clothes to black long dresses."

One of the ways Jews could avoid the growing terror in Czechoslovakia was to isolate themselves, which only increased their economic and social deprivation. As the war progressed, rumors about the situation of the Jews and Poles in the East began to be spread. Either due to their learned helplessness, disbelief or religious faith, the Czech Jews tried to ignore these rumors. One respondent recalls this isolation and spreading rumors:

"I had to spend one day a week going to camp for work, forced labor. The fear of war drew everybody into the home. Jewish people were avoiding exposing themselves, not to be ridiculed."

"We were economically depressed, socially depressed. I was waiting for God to help us. People told us what was going on in Poland but nobody did anything and nobody thought it would happen to them. Besides, they broke down the families and took the men away."

By 1943, the Czech Jews were no better off than the Polish Jews. They were being interned in ghettos before being deported to the extermination sites, which were now accepting all European Jews. Like the ghettos in Poland, these ghettos were crowded, unhygienic and had little food. One survivor remembers that the ghetto he was in had no food, no clothing, no place to take a bath or wash up, and was very crowded. He recalls that they slept on the dirt floor.

> "We were sleeping on the floor-jammed up. Just one blanket we had. Every morning we went out with a bucket to get water. The Germans brought food to the hall. We couldn't cook there. We couldn't wash; we didn't take a bath for 4 weeks."

In addition, in these Ghettos Jews were often put into positions of authority over one another forcing each other to conform to Nazi regulations. One respondent reveals that he was chosen by the Nazis to be a kind of "Jewish policemen" in his ghetto. His role was to watch his own family as well as his neighbors to insure that they did not break any rules. His description of this experience exemplifies the no-win situation in which many of the Jews were placed: they were obliged to comply with the Nazi rules for their behavior which entailed Jews informing on or hurting other Jews, or else risk torture and even death.

> "They made Jews hurt other Jews, made them do it by force. They made children hurt their parents, made them do it by force.... They chose me, they call it the Jewish policeman, to watch the Jews so that they would not leave the yard or not visit neighbors, or not get some food. I had to watch my own family. My first bad experience was I visited a neighbor and they caught me and questioned me about what I was doing with that neighbor. My answer was that I was looking for an aspirin because I had a toothache and these two police officers told me to show them what tooth and I opened my mouth to show them and they knocked half of my teeth out with a rifle. I ran home and they ran after me."

Thus, by 1943–44, the Jews in Czechoslovakia were totally subjugated to despair, hunger, helplessness and hopelessness, and thus, in the eyes of the Nazis, were sufficiently prepared for the next step in the final solution, some destined for extermination others for slave labor and imprisonment in the concentration camps.

FRANCE

France had a large Jewish population due to the fact that many Jews had fled to France before the outbreak of the war to escape persecution. In 1942, the total Jewish population was approximately 300,000, and at least 170,000 were foreign-born (Arendt, 1964).

France, following its occupation by Germany, was given priority by the Nazis to deport their Jews. Until the end of 1942, France cooperated with the Nazis in deporting foreign-born Jews. However, about the end of 1942, Germany requested the deportation of French-born Jews. This request for deportation of their "own" Jews, coupled with rumors coming from abroad that deported Jews were not being resettled but rather murdered, caused the

French to rescind their agreement to cooperate with the Nazis. After 1942, the French helped hide Jews and certain areas in France, particularly the Cote d'Azur became a safe haven for Jews of diverse nationalities. Despite the relative safety of life in the southern part of France, Jews were not immune to being hunted by Nazis. Jews in France encountered similar stresses to those experienced by Jews in other European countries. Families were in fear. Uncertain of their future, they had financial difficulties, and were in constant danger. Survivor participants in our research indicate the changing situations in France at different times:

> "It was very tense, very nervous, and very sad. We lived in one city in France and were told not to live as a family in the same city. We were 40 miles from the German frontier and a very good friend told us to go to the south of France. If something happens to the Jews we would have a chance to save our lives. We left the city with 13 suitcases but left everything but what we could carry ourselves, behind."

> "We had problems, always thinking the Germans will come and get us, since they were in France. We had rations and had to fill out ration cards-we put down that we were Jewish, which was probably a big mistake-that's how the Germans found out about us and traced us from city to city when we had to show our ration cards. At the time, we didn't realize it. We were concerned everyday."

> "One day my mother made an appointment with the dentist (for my sister and me), and my sister and I went to the dentist by bike. When we came back the son of a farmer was waiting for us and said the SS came in a car to take you all away. They took my mother and she told them we had left and she didn't know where we were. They said that they would come back and pick us up. I remember going into the house and the table was set for lunch. We grabbed our clothes and the mayor of the city, who also was a teacher, took my sister and me in his house. At this point I didn't know a thing, my sister told me. He kept us in one of the bedrooms, fed us, and gave us false ID papers. He asked us what name we want and what date of birth. And after 8 or 9 days, people started to talk and got suspicious and the mayor told us we couldn't stay with him any longer. We went to the baker of the village and stayed a few days there. The baker and his nephew were involved in the underground and they and the mayor helped a lot of people that were hiding from the Germans and they knew we were Jewish."

ROMANIA

Romania had a history of being one of the anti-Semitic countries in pre-war Europe (Arendt, 1964; Yahil, 1990). In one of our respondent's view, the country was so very anti-Semitic that it could be smelled for miles. German propaganda, encouraging anti-Semitic activity, only increased the anti-Jewish fervor in Romania. In 1940, the German army entered Romania, and severe anti-Jewish legislation was introduced, jeopardizing the lives of the country's 800,000 Jews. Yahil indicates in his review that grave assaults on the Jews were characteristic of this period. They took the form of both riots and oppressive laws, the most damaging of which was the Jewish Statute is-sued on August 8, 1940. These laws banned Jews from serving in government or public positions, established limits on the number of Jewish students in schools and universities, prohibited Jews from working in publishing and the press, limited the civil rights of the Jews, and even prohibited Jews from converting to Christianity. In October of that year, the confiscation of Jewish property began, following the model practiced in Germany. Jewish-owned land was expropriated, and the Jews were deprived of the right of ownership in all branches of the economy (Yahil, 1990).

When Romania entered the war in February 1941, on the side of the Germans, the fate of the Jews was sealed. Even before deportations could be arranged to the death camps in the East, the Romanian government, under the leadership of the fascist government of Antonescu, authorized the massacre of Romanian Jews. Deportation, Romanian style, consisted of herding thousands of people into freight cars and letting them die of suffocation while the train traveled through the countryside aimlessly for days on end. Romanian concentration camps were established and run by the Romanians themselves because deportation to the East was not feasible. The horrors of these camps were elaborate and atrocious (Arendt, 1964). By August 1942, the Romanians, without the help of the Germans, killed 300,000 Jews. Our survivors remember the debilitating impact these new decrees had on Jewish business and personal lives:

> "We had to wear yellow stars. [We] saw signs which said 'Gentile, don't buy at the Jewish stores.' You were not trusted-with nothing. A Gentile could come to a store and make application to take over the store or business without paying for it. Violent Hungarians gave Jews a rough time. We couldn't fight them because they would take you to the police station and there they would beat you almost to death."

However, by the middle of 1942, the Romanians also realized that saving Jewish lives could be profitable. Curiously, after 1942, Romania became a haven for some wealthy and prominent Jews. As Arendt (1964) indicates the Romanian government had discovered that they could sell Jews abroad for hard currency, so the Romanians became fervent adherents of Jewish emigration-at thirteen hundred dollars a head. This is how Romania came to be one of the few outlets for Jewish emigration to Palestine during the war. And as the Red Army drew nearer, Antonescu became more "moderate." He now was willing to let Jews go without any compensation (Arendt, 1964). Romania can be seen, therefore, as a "fair weather" German ally. When it was to its advantage to deport and slaughter Jews in order to gain German favor, it did so ruthlessly. However, when the tide began to turn against the Germans and the Russian army began its offensive mission, Romania offered some protection for the Jews.

HUNGARY

Hungary joined the war on the side of the Nazis in 1941, mainly in order to gain more property from the neighboring countries of Slovakia, Romania, and Yugoslavia (Yahil, 1990; Arendt, 1964). At that time, the Hungarian government was anti-Semitic, favoring the deportation of all stateless Jews from its newly acquired territories. However, mass deportations from Hungary were premature according to the Nazi overall plan. The Nazis favored systematic deportation of Jews starting from the West, moving toward the East. As a result, Hungary, inadvertently, became a relatively safe place for Jews to reside until March 1944 (Arendt, 1964). In addition, Hungary became a refuge for the Jews who were able to flee persecution from nearby Poland, Czechoslovakia, and Romania. By 1944, the number of Jews residing in Hungary had increased from approximately 500,000 to 800,000 Jews. Yahil (1990) indicates that most of the Jews were actually pleased about coming under Hungarian rule, because in the first phase of the war, it appeared that the Jews of Hungary would be able to hold out even under wartime conditions. They thought that the Hungarian leader Horthy, who was known to be friendly with a number of Jews, would not follow the policies of other anti-Semitic regimes in Europe.

Most of the Hungarian Jewish respondents in our research did not recall anti-Jewish actions until 1944. A few of the respondents, however, report that the restriction of Jewish activities, did begin to occur in 1940. For example, certain professions became closed for Jews and restrictions were placed upon their movements. Yet, at this time, it appears that there were still ways to circumvent the system and blend unobtrusively among the non-Jewish population. Our respondents indicate restriction and limitations on Jewish life and property.

"I was the only Jew, I was working between Gentiles, and heard anti-Semitic remarks, but generally it wasn't that bad."

"I owned a good size agency and had to take in a Gentile partner, that way I could continue my business."

"It was difficult because my father was jailed and I was very fond of my father. There was an accusation against him of different wrong doings, what he really didn't do."

"Everybody called me a dirty Jew. They were trying to make us lose the job because we were Jewish but the owner was a Jew, so I kept the job."

When the Nazis occupied Hungary in 1944, the extermination of the Jews was their intense primary objective. One respondent who was deported to Auschwitz from the ghetto describes the changes, which took place in her life when the Nazis invaded Hungary in 1944:

"As soon as the Germans came over to Hungary, we had a very nice home and that was the very first house that German doctors took over and they gave us one room with no exit and restricted our leaving the place. Our neighbors worried about us and came to the window and told us to come over to live with them. We had an uncle who lived in another city and I called him up and he said he would send a man to take us to his village. It wasn't easy because the Germans were on the road and you needed ID's. The man came with the horse and buggy, filled up with straw and said that during the night he will stop and we should watch out. And one by one, at night, slowly, we went to the buggy and hid under the straw. When we went though, the Germans stopped us but the man was acting drunk and hit the horses hard and he was singing and so the Germans let us go by. We went to the forest till we reached the village. We lived there for two or three months. The family went to the forest and they made a bunker for us to survive in. My uncle gave money to the police, he was a successful businessman, and they all cooperated with him. So they all went to the bunker to live, but I couldn't go because my aunt was sick and I had to help her.

In my town, after the Germans left our house, the mayor was very good to the Jewish people. He gave protection to them and when Jewish people were not allowed to travel, he sent me a permit to travel back to my house, so we could rent it. I had to wear the yellow star when I was on the train to go home and I felt very uneasy with no other Jews around. When I changed trains the police stopped me, but when they saw my permit they let me go. Then came the time when the Nazis took my uncle and cousins. And they said to us we have to go to a small ghetto in the town and they brought some other people from other villages too. In the small ghetto the Hungarian police came to tell us in secret that we would be taken to the big ghetto the next day. We tried to escape, they caught us and took us back and watched us. We were put in the middle of the ghetto. They were watching us all the time."

Whereas previously Hungary had been a relative safe refuge for the Jews, it now became a precarious place to be a Jew. Arendt (1964) indicates that nowhere else were so many people deported and exterminated in such a brief span of time. In less than two months, 147 trains, carrying 434,351 people in sealed freight cars, a hundred persons to a car, left the country, and the gas chambers of Auschwitz were hardly able to cope with this multitude. The last train to leave Hungary for Auschwitz was in the middle of July 1944. By that time, approximately 600,000 Hungarian Jews had been killed.

THE EINSATZGRUPPEN

The Einsatzgruppen, the killing units, conducted the initial enforcement of mass killings directed against those who were viewed to be "anti-German" elements. The first groups of mass victims to be executed were the Russian Jews and Bolsheviks, who were brutally murdered by the Einsatzgruppen in occupied Russia. Documentation of many of the commands given to and subsequent actions taken by members of the Einsatzgruppen are provided by the postwar testimonies of German reserve police battalion members, who assisted the Einsatzgruppen in their gruesome task (Hilberg, 1985).

On July 8th, Heinrich Himmler, Reichsfuhrer SS and chief of German police visited battalions in Bialystok. There, he gave execution orders to the troops. He ordered that all male Jews between the ages of 17 and 45 be convicted as plunderers and to be shot according to martial law. The shootings were to take place away from cities, villages, and thoroughfares. The graves were to be leveled in such a way that no pilgrimage site could arise. He forbade the photographing and the permitting of spectators at the executions. Executions and gravesites were not to be made known (Browning, 1992). One of our survivors from Chernowitz, a town in the Ukraine, remembers hiding as the German troops entered the town and gunned down Jewish members of her community. Those that could went into hiding.

For many Jews, however, hiding provided no long-term protection since they were usually hunted down and killed by the perpetrators. Browning (1992) describes the "Jew hunts" which took place in many forms in Poland. Not only Jews, but also partisans and escaped Russian prisoners of war were targets of these sweeps. Some Jews went into hiding in the forests. The Nazi Einsatzgruppen units searched through the woods and hidden underground bunkers. Those who were found were hauled out. The Jews were then shot on the spot. Other Jews were forced to lie face down on the ground and were shot in the neck. All Jews located in these searches were shot, including men and women of all ages.

Thus in the early stages of the war, shooting, in the form of mass executions, was the norm by which "asocial" elements were to be controlled. However, beginning in December 1941, new and "more efficient" means of killing were initiated—extermination by gas. At that time, the decree ordering the "final solution" of the Jewish question began to be enforced, and the concentration camps became the predominant location for the murder campaign.

THE EXTERMINATION AND CONCENTRATION CAMPS

Mass extermination began at Chelmno on December 8, 1941 and lasted until mid-January 1945. The early exterminations at Chelmno were conducted in gas vans, where approximately one thousand people were murdered each day (Yahil, 1990). Most of the victims during the early stages of operation at Chelmno came from the Lodz district, including many of the inhabitants of the Lodz ghetto (Yahil, 1990).

By the summer of 1942, many more death camps had been set up to work toward a final solution through their murderous activities. Belzec,

Sobibor, Treblinka, and Majdanek were the main death camps located on the eastern border of Poland. While Belzec, Sobibor and Treblinka were used exclusively for extermination, Majdanek functioned as both a work camp and an extermination center (Gilbert, 1982; Yahil, 1990). The other infamous camp, located on the western border of Poland, bordering both Czechoslovakia and Germany was Auschwitz. This camp, perhaps the best known for its atrocities, was both an extermination and concentration center. Much is known about this camp for the reason that this was a selection as well as a concentration camp. Persons arriving at Auschwitz were subjected to the selection process. Those considered able to work were sent to various concentration camps and those too young or too old were send to the gas chambers and than were cremated.

Dachau, Buchenwald, Sachsenhausen, Flossenburg, Mauthausen, and Ravensbruck (a women's camp) were some of the well-known concentration camps, located within the bounds of the Reich. Although these camps were not used exclusively for extermination, many Jews perished in these camps as a result of the atrocious living and work conditions (Hilberg, 1985).

At the beginning of the war, forced labor was used as a means of extermination. However, as the war intensified, the Germans realized that they needed workers to help in the war effort. The decision was made to use the strongest and most able concentration camp prisoners for physical labor. Despite the exploitation of camp inmates for their labor, the goal of "the final solution" remained central to Nazi policy. Jews who were selected to work were eventually to be annihilated (Yahil, 1990). In other words, employment was not an alternative plan for the prisoners; it was a temporary occurrence, which could be exploited before the prisoners were to be executed (Weiss, 1996).

Mauthausen provides one example of a distribution and labor camp. Few prisoners sent to Mauthausen labor camp survived. Located near a rock/granite quarry, the camp was established so that cheap prisoner labor could excavate the building materials to be used for Hitler's grandiose architectural building schemes. According to Eckstein (1978), Mauthausen was intended for prisoners for whom there was no prospect of being brought back into the fold. This meant that the transfer of a prisoner to Mauthausen was tantamount to a death sentence. Even when the camp was first built, work in the Mauthausen quarry was carried out by the most primitive and brutal methods, which led to death of prisoners in a very short period of time.

Pawelczynska (1979), a survivor of Auschwitz, writes that workers in Auschwitz faced not only a constant threat of severe beatings and killing, but also low morale, since the work itself was actually used to break the spirit of the worker:

"The possibility of surviving was reduced to a minimum by inability to work together and to work in self-defense against biological annihilation through hard labor. Those who did not believe the experiences of their companions, and thought their hard work would be appreciated by the agents of authority, lost their last reserves of strength and dropped to the bottom of the camp community." (Pawelczynska, 1979:63).

The number of camps increased between 1942 and 1944. Dora-Mittelbau and Riga-Kaiserwald were both established in 1943. Bergen-Belsen, established first as a transit and exchange camp for Jews holding foreign passports, became an authorized concentration camp in 1944. Aside from these better known camps, there were other camps established during the war period, which were used as transit, labor or security centers (Weiss, 1996).

Many of the survivors in our research went through the selection process and were incarcerated in Auschwitz for a period of time. The stresses endured in Auschwitz were manifold. They included physical, emotional, psychological and social turmoil. The Nazis were ruthless in their quest to kill, and hiding from them proved to be a major stress for the hunted Jews. Other survivors were interned at several other concentration camps, including Bergen-Belsen, Buchenwald, Dora, Dachau, Gusen, Ebensee, and Theresienstadt.

Personal accounts of survivor participants in this research reveal that there was a great deal of instability during the war years; few of the survivors stayed in any one camp or place for more than a few months. These survivors may have been among the strongest of the prisoners and it was their strength that enabled them to endure the harsh slave labor conditions and survive.

LIFE IN HIDING AND IN THE CONCENTRATION CAMPS

A few respondents described the terror of their hiding. One survivor describes her close call with the Gestapo while she was hiding in a Ukrainian village:

"At the end of March 1944, the Russians were not far from our town, we escaped from our camp at night. The Ukrainian peasants waited for us—they had other people hidden too. One of the peasants was in danger too. He used to deliver forty loaves of bread. Ten people were there when the Germans retreated around the building where we were hidden in an attic under the roof and we sat very still so that they would not discover us. It was terrible, the flies all over. We were in danger all the time. The Gestapo looked there for workers. Once one of the girls there got so upset, she started to cry and we had to keep her quiet so the Gestapo wouldn't hear her."

This respondent demonstrates the vulnerability of interpersonal relationships and the stresses these relationships had to endure in the oppressive context of man-hunts. The individuals who helped hide or care for those in hiding placed their own lives in danger. They could be shot on the spot or sent to concentration camps for their role in protecting others. Browning (1992) describes the testimony of an eyewitness, in which the German policy for shooting those who aided the Jews was disclosed. He indicates that tips from Polish informants often instigated the "Jew hunts". The Germans systematically shot Poles who provided lodging to Jews. Almost always they also burned down their lodging.

Hiding was a trying ordeal; any sound could reveal the hiding place of the group and the fear of being surrounded and closed in upon by the "hunters" may have caused any individual to emotionally break under the pressure. Others in hiding had no recourse to help. They had to quickly become self-sufficient. One survivor describes her experiences of hiding in the forest of Krakow, Poland, for nine months. She reveals the problem of losing trust in others since deceptive tricks were used to get Jews to come out of hiding. Informers betrayed both the whereabouts of the Jews and the helpful actions of their Polish rescuers:

"It was very difficult. We had to run away at night all the time and had to look for food during the night and often went without food. We had to find places where to sleep. Under a tree or wherever we found a place. It was difficult to exist, the uncertainty if someone comes by and kills us."

"There were about 245–250 people hiding and I am the only one left alive. I ran from forest to forest, the underground Poles killed most of the Jews in the forest, the Germans were afraid to go in deep. I just kept running. We had made bunkers. There was a Polish police officer that was friends with my brother-in-law. He made a hiding place for us under a barn. He made a hole that could be closed. But the other Poles were after him where he kept the Jews. There were notices on the trees that Jews should come out of hiding. They will be forgiven. Some Jews thought they meant it and they came out and went to that city. Two weeks later they sent whomever they caught to Treblinka. I ran away again, jumped a tall fence to that hiding place. We lost one half of the people in our group at that time. Later, we stayed in the forest. When spring came, water came in and we had to get out and a gentleman let us go in the attic of his house and about 15 people went there. Then some people came to his house and said we would be killed. Then they started to chase us, including my oldest sister and brother-in-law. They knocked a pregnant woman over the forehead with a hatchet. My oldest sister grabbed me with her hand and said, "let's run away" and we threw ourselves into a bush. It was pure luck. Germans run around with dogs looking for Jews, most of them killed already. We went again into the forest to hide in the same place. I had a cousin who knew we were hiding. He paid a Polish man to bring us back to the ghetto. So I said "I am not leaving". That same night they took 19 boys and burned them and put them in the hole. One boy came back naked and I gave him clothes. He went back to Keltze ghetto with one eye. They started shooting at us from all sides that night and one man cursed us in Polish. I was the only one left. Still, I didn't know how I survived. I walked back to our city 50 km away. That guy with the one eye sneaked me in for work in a camp. The Poles were so barbaric."

Another survivor who assumed a different identity as a means of hiding from the Nazis relates a slightly different form of hiding experience. From 1941–1945 she lived in Warsaw, acting as a native Catholic Pole. She recounts that assuming this identity was extremely stressful, especially practicing a religion that was foreign to her and establishing convincing relationships based on a falsified past. It was her fluency in the Polish language, which enabled her to successfully survive this ordeal:

> "When I came to Warsaw I wanted to take care of children. My first job was working as a maid, a babysitter. In order to work in the outside you needed to be listed on the employment ranks. After this job I had another job as a salesperson in a food store only for Germans and very important Poles. I had this job until 1945. It was one problem after another. It was a big fight. I was trying to be one of them. It was a continuation of telling one lie after another about family and friends, about things I did in the past. Adopting their religion, going to church everyday, and for a while, even believing in their God, that He can do more than my God did. I came once home from work in Warsaw. Two policemen were standing by the gate of the apartment and asked for my identification card. They took me away to the police station in a jeep. There they told me that they suspected I was Jewish and I should tell them if this was the truth. I was hit a couple of times on my back with a belt and I screamed real loud that I was not Jewish. They let me go home. That's what saved me- the card and the language too."

LIBERATION

The defeat of Nazi Germany brought an end to the physical assaults and brutalities inflicted on Jews. Over six million Jews were murdered during the World War II years. It is estimated that about one half million survived the Holocaust living in Europe. As indicated earlier in this chapter, survivors of the Holocaust vary in terms of their wartime experiences. There were those who managed to escape and lived through the war years in Great Britain and Sweden and were consequently better off. Likewise, those who survived in Bulgaria, Italy and Siberia had less traumatic experiences. Those who were in hiding or with resistance groups lived in a state of constant fear. Survivors who were liberated from concentration camps were barely alive. They suffered from malnutrition and debilitating illnesses.

The above description focused on those actually engaged in the aggressive actions and atrocities during the war years. In addition, these were criticized in various countries who may be classified as bystanders (Hillberg, 1992). These individuals ranged from bystanders sympathetic to the Nazis but not actively involved in the brutalities, to those sympathetic, to the persecuted but too fearful for their own lives to take any action on their behalf. At the end of WWII, the Nazis and their allies were defeated. But the days of liberation did not offer a welcome to the survivors (Dinnerstein, 1982).

They were rejected by their countries of origin and had to settle as displaced persons, since entry to lands of freedom was closed to them.

The aftermath of liberation brought about three challenges for the survivors. First, survivors had to come to terms with their own survival. Many were in such bad physical condition that it took them months to regain some semblance of health. Second, they had to try and find family members who survived. Most survivors realized that they lost most of their family members and friends and they had to begin and come to terms with their losses. Third, they had to try and establish new lives in yet another location which entailed many obstacles and challenges.

REFERENCES

Arendt, H. (1976). *Eichman in Jerusalem: A Report on the Banality of Evil.* New York: Penguin Books.

Bauer, Y. & Rotenstreich, N. (1981). *The Holocaust as Historical Experience.* New York: Holmes and Meier.

Browning, C.R. (1992). *The Path to Genocide: Essays on Launching the Final Solution.* New York, NY: Cambridge University Press.

Dinnerstein, L. (1982). *America and the Survivors of the Holocaust.* New York: Columbia University Press.

Eckstein, B. (1978). The Austrian civil population knew what happened in the concentration camps, *Yalkut Moreshet Periodical,* 26, 187–189.

Gilbert, M. (1982). *The MacMillan Atlas of the Holocaust.* New York: MacMillan.

Gill, A. (1988). *The Journey Back From Hell: An Oral History. Conversations with Concentration Camp Survivors.* New York: Morrow.

Goldhagen, D.J. (1996). *Hitler's Willing Executioners: Ordinary Germans and the Holocaust.* New York: Knopf.

Hilberg, R. (1985). *The Destruction of the European Jews.* New York: Holmes & Meier.

Hillberg, R. (1992). *Perpetrators, Victims, Bystanders: The Jewish Catastrophe 1933–1945.* New York: Harper-Collins Publishers.

Morrison, J.G. (2000). *Ravensbruck: Everyday Life in a Women's Concentration Camp 1939–1945.* Princeton, NJ: Marcus Wiener.

Pawelczynska (1979). *Values and Violence in Auschwitz: A Sociological Analysis.* Berkeley: University of California Press.

Weiss, J. (1996). *Ideology of Death: Why the Holocaust Happened in Germany.* Chicago, IL: I.R. Dee.

Yahil, L. (1990). *The Holocaust: the fate of European Jewry.* New York: Oxford Press.

3

From Destruction To Search
For New Lives

INTRODUCTION

This chapter reviews the experiences of survivors in their quest to establish new lives, following their liberation from the horrendous experiences during the Holocaust years. As indicated in the previous chapter, over six million Jews perished at the hands of the Nazis. The Allied Forces liberated fewer than 200,000 survivors at various concentration camps in Germany and Austria (Harel, Biegel, & Guttman, 1994). There are extensive historical accounts of the Holocaust period, which most certainly constituted a unique period in the annals of human history (Bauer, 1982; Lookstein, 1985; Wyman, 1984).

Holocaust survivors varied in terms of how they spent the war years. Some managed to escape in the early stages of the Nazi rule. Others were in ghettoes or in concentration camps. Some survivors went into hiding. There were survivors who spent the war years with resistance groups. While some survivors were only in one such type of situation, others were successively in more than one traumatic setting. These may have included being in a ghetto first, then in hiding or in a number of different camps (Kahana, Harel & Kahana, 1988).

Approximately 150,000 Holocaust survivors who were liberated from concentration camps returned to their countries of origin, which included Belgium, Holland, France, Czechoslovakia, Hungary, Poland, and Yugoslavia (Bauer, 1982). Approximately 175,000 Jews from Poland, who fled from the Nazi invasion and spent the war years in Russia, returned in 1946 to Poland. Survivors of the Holocaust, regardless of their circumstances, have suffered and endured personal and material losses during the Holocaust years. In addition to personal hardships which they endured, they also lost family members and friends and opportunities for educational and personal development. Upon return to their countries of origin, they were faced with environments that were, at best, indifferent to their suffering and, in most instances, openly hostile.

Many of the survivors who returned to their countries of origin following liberation, decided very soon to seek new lives elsewhere. Two primary reasons compelled them not to stay in their prior homelands. First, there were too many bad memories of their earlier life experiences. Memories of lost family members and friends haunted them and had made their stay difficult. Second, there were clear, unmistakable signs of anti-Semitism all around them. They encountered these signs at every step: as they were trying to reclaim their own homes and family possessions, as they searched for employment or as they attempted to establish new business ventures. There were two primary new destinations selected by survivors: the United States and Israel. However, entry into either one of those two countries, immediately after the war, was virtually impossible.

This chapter reviews survivor responses to open ended questions. First, experiences of survivors in the immediate aftermath of the Holocaust, in their countries of origin and in displaced persons (D.P.) camps in Austria and Germany are reviewed. Second, sources of assistance, which aided survivors in the D.P. camps in their quest for immigration, are identified. Third, factors that determined immigration to the U.S. and Israel are reviewed. Fourth, differences in environmental characteristics, stressors and challenges which survivors experienced in their new environments conclude the chapter.

AFTER LIBERATION

As Hitler masterminded and carried out the extermination of Jews throughout Europe, he had much willing help inside and outside of Germany. The Holocaust may be seen, therefore, as the collective accomplishment of Europe of those days. The willing help of European governments and the indifference of Western democracies, especially of the world powers, served to reassure Hitler and his associates that there would be no interference with the implementation of their malevolent plans and barbaric actions. The deportation and extermination of Jewish people was facilitated not only by the acquiescence of governments and religious leadership but also by active assistance of local populations. The Pope, the religious leadership and the neutral countries stood by without speaking out or acting on behalf of six million humans who were slaughtered by the Nazis. The countries which could have accepted Jewish refugees, including the U.S., refused to expand their quota system or change their immigration policies, leaving these survivors in a state of nowhere to turn to (Hilberg, 1985).

During the World War II years, anti-Semitism served as an important factor in the U.S. reaction, or more appropriately stated non-reaction, to the plight of Jews in Europe. Anti-Semitic feelings and sentiments flourished in the U.S. during the WWII years (Dinnerstein, 1982; Wyman, 1984). There were numerous acts of vandalism, desecration of synagogues and cemeteries, and outbreaks of attacks against Jews. There were also widespread, hate-filled expressions of hostility against the Jews, written to U.S. government officials and congressional representatives, in opposition to the admission of Jewish refugees to the U.S. The configuration of open and passive anti-Semitism brought about the sentiment of an overwhelming majority of the population not to care about European Jews, nor to care whether the U.S. government did anything to help save them. Anti-Semitism was also widespread in the military forces and among those who worked in refugee camps (Bauer, 1982). In a report to President Truman concerning the D.P. camps in Germany, Earl G. Harrison, presidential representative to the Intergovernmental committee on Refugees, stated that the American military were treating the Jews as did the Nazis except that we do not exterminate them." (Nachmani, 1986; p. 1).

These attitudes and sentiments constituted significant factors and reduced the likelihood that the U.S. would develop initiatives to save Jews during the WWII years and to offer them assistance in the aftermath of the Holocaust. Policymakers and government officials viewed the potential rescue of Jews as an unnecessary burden or danger which was best to be avoided rather than taken on.

It has been estimated that approximately 6,000,000 Jews were murdered or perished during the Holocaust. Almost half of them were Polish Jews. Of the Jews who survived WWII in Europe, approximately 400,000 were either displaced persons who were forcibly evicted from their homes, or refugees who remained or returned to their native countries (Nachmani, 1986). After the end of World War II, some Holocaust survivors returned to their countries of origin to seek out surviving family members. They expected that their stressful experiences and losses during the World War II years would be followed by understanding and support from the citizens in their countries of origin. However, there was no such sympathy or understanding forthcoming. Those who returned from concentration camps, former ghetto fighters, those who served with resistance groups, and/or those who survived in hiding, upon their return to their hometowns, were faced with social environments ranging from open hostility and overt anti-Semitism to casual indifference. In addition, they were haunted by memories of their persecution both prior to and during the Holocaust, including the memories of lost family members and friends. Many survivors decided that they could not reestablish themselves in the environments from which they were driven away and where open anti-Semitism was still practiced.

Approximately 65,000 Holocaust survivors who were liberated from concentration camps in Austria and Germany decided to stay there. Those who stayed and those who returned to Austria and Germany from their countries of origin believed that they would be able to get from there to new destinations. When survivors began to explore possible new destinations where they could start new lives, they came to realize that access to the United States was denied to them by immigration quota restrictions. The British government also closed immigration to Israel, which was called at that time 'Palestine'. In the absence of other alternatives, survivors settled in displaced persons (D.P.) camps, hoping that immigration to the U.S. or Israel would eventually become possible.

At the end of World War II, displaced persons in Europe, numbered over seven million individuals living primarily in the occupied territories in Germany and Austria. They included former slave laborers brought in from Eastern Europe to work in German farms and factories, former prisoners-of-war (P.O.W.), survivors of concentration camps, and Eastern Europeans who either came voluntarily to help the Germans or fled the advancing Russian armies in 1944 (Dinnerstein, 1982).

THE DISPLACED PERSONS (D.P.) CAMPS

Responses of participants to open ended questions in our research indicate that, for many survivors, Austria, Germany and Italy served as initial countries of entry and as locations of transition for immigration to other countries. Between the end of WWII and the summer of 1946, hundreds of Jews were murdered either individually or in pogroms in Poland. This brought about an increased realization on the part of many Holocaust survivors that life in post-war Poland was treacherous, and anything but secure. Following the post-war pogrom in Kielce in which 42 Jews were murdered, approximately 100,000 Jews fled Poland and adjacent countries and settled in the American and British sectors of Germany (Bauer, 1982).

It was evident from the majority of responses to our interviews that few respondents, if any, intended to make Germany their home. Austria, as well, became a location for transition, as did Italy for a smaller number. These countries were hardly a preferred "choice" for those survivors who remained or returned there. Some of our respondents stated that they either did not want to return to their country of origin or that after returning there they were driven away either because of hostilities or they just felt that they could not stay there due to their emotional and psychological reactions and traumatic memories. The following examples are illustrative of our respondents' feelings towards their countries of origin and their reasons for settling in displaced persons camps:

"Because I didn't want to stay in Poland where all my family got murdered";

"I was liberated in Austria and had no one to go back to in Poland";

"The American army was there. It was more secure. In Poland there was still anti-Semitism";

"We had no choice. We had to get out of Poland because of anti-Semitism and pogroms and going to Austria meant perhaps going to Israel from there";

"Austria was the only place I could go to. Couldn't go from Poland to the U.S";

"Seeing the stones chased me out. My whole family was killed in Poland. I couldn't stay and live there";

"I was unwelcome in Poland. The Russians did nothing to help either";

"Because of anti-Semitism and the pogroms in Poland";

"The DP camps were the places where I could stay";

"I left Poland because of the pogroms and Austria was the closest country where I could go to."

As the responses of participants in our research indicate, the DP camps were viewed as an alternative living place to their countries of origin. Quite a few found the conditions in the displaced persons camps in Austria and Germany more favorable than those in Poland. In Poland, discrimination and persecutions were becoming prevalent again. Because of hostilities, anti-Semitism and/or pogroms in their countries of origin, D.P. camps became a more desirable alternative as temporary residences for many survivors. Some respondents stated that, since the American army was there, it was more secure. Other survivors stayed in the camps to begin with or returned to them from their countries of origin because they felt that they had no other alternatives. In response to questions about their reasons for entering D.P. camps, typical responses were:

"I had no other choice. There was no place to go. The D.P. camp was in Germany";

"I had to. The D.P. camps were there. There was nowhere else I could go";

"I found my sister in Poland and I didn't find other family [members]. This was the only country we could go to and from there we could maybe go on";

"We were sent there after crossing Polish border";

"I could stay there. I did not want to. There was Jewish blood everywhere";

"Camps were made in Germany for people who wanted to live there";

"Due to a friend's suggestion who was with us in the camp";

"I didn't want to. In Hungary the Russians were in control and we did not want to stay there";

"It was not far from Ludwigsdorf where I was liberated";

"Crossed the border and was brought there by Americans occupying Germany";

"I was in a DP camp from 1946 until 1947 in Germany. Had no other place to go";

"Got back to Germany and stayed in a DP camp for one year."

IMMIGRATION ASSISTANCE IN DISPLACED PERSONS (D.P.) CAMPS

Displaced Persons' camps, provided living environments not just for Jewish Holocaust survivors but also for other refugees who feared or did not wish to return to their homelands. Many survivors were attempting to locate relatives in the D.P. camps or were hoping to secure American protection, if not sponsorship. Some Jewish organizations used Germany as a place of transition in aiding individuals to go to Israel. This was especially true of the "Bricha," which was an organization formed in Poland by Jewish soldiers who served in the Jewish Brigade and survived the Holocaust. They assisted people to leave Poland and directed them towards Palestine, the place where they wanted to establish a Jewish homeland. Bricha helped those who wanted to immigrate to Israel to cross borders and get to areas in Germany, Austria and Italy which served as staging areas for immigration to the Jewish homeland.

From the Displaced Persons (D.P.) camps, immigration was being arranged to Palestine. Survivors wanted to get to these camps and wait there until they could receive visas or would be able to continue toward their ultimate destination. An estimated 250,000 Holocaust survivors were aided by the Bricha in their flight from their respective countries to get to Germany, Austria and Italy. However, not all of Holocaust survivors who were in the D.P. camps wanted to go to Israel. A significant number among them hoped to reach the U.S., especially those with family members who immigrated there prior to WWII.

Immediately after liberation, the Jewish Brigade, which was part of the British army, started to seek out and help survivors. Many of those who served with the Jewish Brigade were also members of the Jewish underground, the Haganah. In army trucks, marked by the Jewish Star of David and the blue and white national colors, they visited camps to help survivors organize and to help those who wanted to immigrate to Palestine. The activities of the

Bricha and those of the Jewish Brigade were coordinated by a branch of the Jewish Agency that constituted the Government of the State of Israel in formation. Responses of the survivors who participated in our research provide examples of their views of life in the D.P. camp as a temporary arrangement on the way to Israel or to the U.S. Examples of their views are offered below:

"Because we intended to go to Israel from there";

"D.P. camp, transit, stayed there on the way to Israel";

"I wanted to go to Israel and that was the way to get there";

"We were on the way to Israel".

"Bricha group helped us and they put us up in a transit camp. These were all the transit people who wanted to get to Palestine. This was temporary. My sister was only member of the family with me";

"Our entire kibbutz group moved to Germany on the way to Israel";

"B'nai Brith took me from Czechoslovakia to there and then to West Germany, where my brother and I helped smuggling people across borders on the way to Israel";

"The Movement sent me to open up the road to Italy through the Alps";

"Transition to either Palestine or US I wanted to get to Israel";

"I was leading Jews toward Israel. They were going to Israel from Italy";

"Because I was liberated there and was waiting to go to Israel."

The D.P. camps were also the locales where applications could be made at that time to immigrate to the U.S. A significant number of survivors were in D.P. camps waiting for their application to be processed and for their entry visas to arrive:

"Germany was a stopping point to go to America";

"Because I knew U.S. soldiers were there and [there was] a chance to get to America";

"Because from Germany we knew that we could go to U.S. or to another free country";

"Had to go there to get to U.S. We wanted to go to the United States";

"I went there to be closer to America";

"That was the only place I could emigrate from to the U.S.";

"To immigrate to another country, and maybe to America."

Shortly after the end of World War II, the United Nations Relief and Rehabilitation Administration (U.N.R.R.A.), along with the Red Cross and other organizations, initiated efforts to aid refugees in their transition and resettlement needs. The American Joint Distribution Committee (J.D.C.), the Jewish Agency and other Jewish relief organizations supplemented these efforts in order to meet the needs of Holocaust survivors and other Jewish refugees in D.P. camps. Throughout Germany and Austria, there were the displaced persons (D.P.) camps that offered primarily food and shelter for survivors and other refugees. Many of the D.P. camps were on the same or adjacent grounds to what previously were concentration/extermination camps.

The accommodation in most of the camps was in open ward style barracks, where individuals had very little privacy and their life space was comprised of a bed and limited closet space. Food in the D.P camps was centrally prepared and distributed. Minimal health services were available, either in the camps or in nearby locations. The following examples illustrate life in the D.P. camps. One of the D.P. camps was at Bergen Belsen. This setting, adjacent to a former concentration camp by that name, provided accommodations for military personnel stationed there during the WWII years. One woman, liberated at Bergen Belsen at age 22, after three years in various camps, describes her life in the Bergen Belsen displaced persons camp as follows:

> "My father, two brothers and one sister were murdered by the Nazis at Auschwitz. My mother and another sister of mine perished in one of the camps where we were together. I had no one to go home to, and I had an uncle in the United States. So I came to Bergen Belsen because I thought that I'd get from there easier to the U.S.;
>
> "I was in the Bergen Belsen D.P. camp for two years waiting for my entry visa to the U.S. to arrive. I was on 'schpilkes' (pins and needles) all that time, waiting to be given permission to join my uncle's family in the U.S."
>
> There wasn't much to do in the camp. We had what (food) to eat and where (place) to sleep, but that was about it. Some of the guys had dealings in Cele, a town that was about 30 kilometers away, but I didn't want to go there because I didn't want to fool around with them and get in trouble. There were some classes where you could learn to read and speak Hebrew or English and you could also learn some sewing;
>
> I just had to wait, and wait, and wait! I would go every week once or twice to check if my papers had come, and I was running out of patience. Finally, after two years, I've got my papers to go to the U.S."

A young man who was 17 years old when he was liberated from Buchenwald, after three and a half years in various ghettoes and camps, returned to Czechoslovakia after the end of the war. When he found out that none of his family members survived he decided to try and immigrate to the U.S. He wandered around in various D.P. camps in Austria and Germany until he decided to settle in the D.P. camp in Bergen Belsen. There, with the assistance of American Jewish Distribution Committee officials, he got in touch with an uncle in Brooklyn, New York and settled into the routine of waiting for the arrival of his entry visa. He describes his experiences there:

"Life in Bergen Belsen was terrible. You had nothing to do all day long or in the evenings. You could not work and earn money. They gave you what to eat and you had a bed to sleep in but nothing more.

They had some 'mickey mouse' classes, but it was just kids' stuff. The only thing you could do is get involved in the black market, buy stuff and sell it. I made some money in buying and selling jewelry. That is how I got my start in the jewelry business. After more than one year in Bergen Belsen, I got tired waiting for my visa and decided to go to Palestine. But that was also not so simple."

Another man was liberated at Mauthausen concentration camp, at the age of 19, after surviving three years in various concentration camps in Austria. He returned to his hometown in Poland, where he started to consider picking up the pieces of his life and learning a trade. However, very soon after his arrival there, he concluded that he did not see a future for himself in Poland. He decided to leave for Germany, with the intention of immigrating to Palestine. He wandered around in various D.P. camps until he joined a Zionist "hachshara" (youth group) in the Landsberg D.P. camp, which was preparing Holocaust survivors for kibbutz life in Israel. He shares his wandering days:

"Until I got to Landsberg, I've been to several other camps. All of them were rotten. People were just waiting around for a way to get to Israel or get an entry visa to the U.S. But other than waiting, there was nothing to do.

With the hachshara group, life was a lot better organized. We had every day Hebrew classes and vocational training. We also had a social life of our own. I don't know how I would have survived life in the D.P. camp if I had not become a member of the group."

Another man was liberated at Ebensee concentration camp, at the age of 19, after four years in various camps in Poland, Germany and Austria. He returned to his hometown in Poland, where he wanted to resettle. Very soon after his arrival there, however, he encountered hostility from his Polish neighbors and threats to his life. One night, when he returned home late, three persons were waiting by his house with clubs ready to assault him. The next day he decided to leave Poland for Germany, with the intention of immigration to Palestine. He wandered around in various D.P. camps until he joined a Zionist youth group in the Bergen Belsen D.P. camp.

"When I was liberated in Ebensee, my first instinctive action was to head home to find out if any members of my family survived. When I got to Warsaw, I found out from a cousin that the Nazis murdered my parents, my brothers and sisters in various camps. I did go to my hometown anyway because I did not know what else to do.

The two months that I spent there were terrible. Every street corner reminded me of death, destruction and suffering. I was still determined to make it a go of it there, until one night, when I went home, I saw three hooligans waiting for me by the side of my house. I got two of my buddies and we beat up on them and broke their bones. I knew then that we did not have a future there. The next day, with the help of the Kovner (Bricha) group, we started on our way to Germany, going through Czechoslovakia and

Austria. I settled in Bergen Belsen, where I got involved with the Beitar movement and
they promised to help me get 'illegally' to Israel."

There were individuals who stayed in D.P. camps in Germany for years.
One man was liberated in Poland at the age of 22 after five years in ghettoes,
hiding, and resistance groups. He went to Germany, wandered around for
several months until he settled into a D.P. camp near Munich. He managed
to get a job with the American Red Cross as a driver and took up permanent residence in the D.P. camp. There he met his wife, also a survivor of
concentration camps. They got married and their first child was born there.
His wife also found a job and they were close to a decision to settle there,
but signs of renewed anti-Semitism convinced them to seek opportunities
for entry into the U.S., which they eventually did, with the assistance of the
American Red Cross. He shares his memories from those days. Note that
one of the persistent themes in these personal accounts is the pervasive
antiJewish behavior of the citizens of these European countries.

"For us life in the D.P. camp has become fairly routine and we thought that we had it,
there, pretty good. We had our own little cocoon, we were young and we did not know
any better. After years in the ghettoes, in hiding, with the partisans, and in the camps,
we thought that we had it made. We made good money and the Germans didn't bother
us. We even started to forget about all the terrible things we lived through. Our Bruce
was born there and he gave us a lot of pleasure. Only when the signs of anti-Semitism
started to show up did we decide not to stay in Germany. We were near ready to look for
an apartment in Munich and to settle there."

OTHER SOURCES OF ASSISTANCE IN D.P. CAMPS

Holocaust survivors who participated in our research indicated they received considerable assistance from various sources while in the D.P. camps.
Respondents from the U.S. indicated considerably higher assistance received from family members than did survivors in our Israeli sample. It
is possible that those with family connections in the U.S. were more likely to
seek assistance from them and to ask for their assistance in securing entry
visas to the U.S. Respondents from the U.S. survivor sample compared with
the Israeli survivors received more assistance from Jewish organizations.
A similar number of respondents indicated receiving assistance from the
American Jewish Joint Distribution Committee (JDC), the Jewish Agency,
and from Jewish vocational and social organizations. Survivors who came
to the U.S. utilized substantial services from the Hebrew Immigrant Aid
Society (H.l.A.S.), the organization that aided them with immigration to
the U.S. Other Jewish organizations mentioned include the Jewish Brigade,
Bricha, and Aliyah Beth. These organizations offered assistance with return

to Germany, with the management of life in the D.P. camps, and with immigration to Palestine. Some survivors also mentioned receiving assistance from Zionist organizations and from Kibbutz movements.

Holocaust survivors also received assistance from non-Jewish organizations. Holocaust survivors from our U.S. sample received more assistance from non-Jewish relief and other organizations than those from the Israeli sample. Respondents indicated that they have received assistance from the United Nations Relief and Rehabilitation Administration (U.N.R.R.A), the International Refugee Organization (I.R.O), the Red Cross, the American Army and the Swedish Government. Assistance was also received from some Christian families and from other sources of support.

FROM THE D.P. CAMPS TO THE UNITED STATES

Anti-Semitic sentiments and actions continued to shape the U.S. inaction concerning Holocaust survivors at the end of World War II. During the WWII years American Jewish leadership encountered outright refusals, and various forms of unsympathetic responses to their concerns from elected representatives and public officials. Only in early 1945 was a War Refugee Board established for the purpose of rescuing endangered people in Europe. The end of the war saw a return to earlier tendencies of indifference, especially towards the plight of Jewish Holocaust survivors. The American government and the U.S. Congress deliberately chose not to act decisively to save European Jewry during WWII or after the war ended. Much of the public was uninformed, and those who were informed, were indifferent (Dinnerstein, 1982).

The American Jewish leadership, which during the nineteen-thirties and the early forties was for the most part timid, disorganized, and concerned about not provoking more intense hostility, has met with limited success in fostering congressional and/or governmental action on behalf of European Jewry (Dinnerstein; 1982). Only towards the end of WWII, with the realization of the magnitude of the Nazi atrocities, has the leadership of Jewish organizations succeeded to unite their efforts and organize to provide emergency and temporary relief for Jewish refugees in Europe, develop political support for the establishment of a Jewish homeland in Palestine, and campaign for increasing the immigration quotas to allow for Jewish Holocaust survivors to immigrate to the U.S. (Dinnerstein, 1982; Wyman, 1984). It is against this background of Jewish efforts and congressional resistance and governmental inaction that Holocaust survivors were spending time in the D.P. camps anxiously awaiting the progress of these negotiations. The limitations in immigration quotas resulted in issuing of a small numbers of entry visas. Between March 31, 1946 and June 30, 1948, 25,594 visas were issued to Jews in D.P. camps in Germany (Dinnerstein, 1982). Overall, during the years of 1945 to 1953, only 176,500 Jewish Holocaust survivors arrived in the United States and Canada (Helmreich, 1990).

When asked why the U.S. was chosen as their destination of immigration, most respondents listed family connections, exigencies, choice by default, or the fulfillment of their vision of the United States as a Promised Land. Most family connections seemed to consist of parents, aunts, uncles, cousins or other relatives. Close kin were most instrumental in securing connections and making arrangements, while secondary kin often sent affidavits. Other sources of aid arose from marriage and/or the spouse's family. Siblings often played a major role, especially if they were already established as U.S. residents. Survivors shared their reasons for choosing the United States and their sources of assistance as exemplified below:

"My parents made the choice. My mother's sister and family were there";

"Thank God my father had enough sense. He accepted a friend's advice";

"My parents chose. We had cousins in the U.S. and my dad was promised a job there";

"My father received an offer to become a professor of chemistry";

"I had a sister who was living already in the U.S.";

"My Father had a brother in the U.S. He had kept in contact with him over the years";

"Because we had two uncles and my husband had a brother in the U.S.";

"In the U.S. my husband had an aunt and I did too. They paid our expenses and we came. My father had a brother in the U.S. before I was born. I told them I had relatives in Detroit. The captain who went to the U.S. had their address and found them. They invited me here";

"To marry my husband who was already in the U.S.";

"My sister was here already; I came for her wedding and stayed";

"My sister got married in Canada, moved to the U.S.";

"We couldn't become French citizens so we tried the U.S.";
"I got an affidavit from relatives. In the U.S. we had family";

"It was the most logical move and we had relatives here that provided the affidavits";

"Because I had good friends, who sent me affidavit";

For some, the choice was of a more emotional nature and for a few, fate intervened, as the following cases illustrate:

"We wanted to go to Israel, but my husband wanted to go to the United States. I could not physically or emotionally stand losing him;

"There was someone in America who sponsored people who would be able to go to America and we were selected";

For those whose first preference was another location (such as Israel), the United States became the destination by default. Other countries did not offer visas to applicants, whereas the quota system of the U.S. would let some through. Fearing being entrapped if they waited longer in the camp, they took the first visa to come through from the U.S. Children, pregnancy, health problems, or safety issues precluded a large number of immigrants from pursuing Israel (their first choice) as a realistic destination:

"Because of all those threats against Israel, I came to the U.S.";

"I could not go to Israel because of pregnancy";

"My second child was born, and I couldn't come to terms with the possibility of war. Nasser used all those threats against Israel";

"I was afraid of another Holocaust. I wanted to go to Israel but my wife didn't want to";

"No freedom in Romania. Started passport application in 1950, denied 3 times";

"I had no choice. The only place I could go because I was able to secure a visa";

"I had no choice. It was the only country I got a visa to";

"There was no other way. All other doors were closed";

For others, the United States represented a kind of "golden dream" a place of freedom and democracy; an embodiment of the Promised Land. In virtually all of the responses in this category, the U. S. was referred to in broad, glowing, symbolic terms such as "the land of opportunity," or, "the greatest country in the world," or, " . . . a free country and we wanted a better tomorrow," The following examples demonstrate these sentiments.

"I always wanted to come here, seemed like it was the Promised Land";

"It was everybody's dream; refuge, haven, land of opportunity";

"It was a free country and we wanted a better tomorrow";

"Since I was a child, I wanted to come to America, to the land of opportunity";

"Because all my life I heard that the U.S. was the best country, and it's true";

"Everybody knows in the U.S. you can live a free life";

"I felt it was the greatest country in the world";

"Because it was a golden dream to come true";

FROM THE D.P. CAMPS TO PALESTINE

Because the British government chose to close Palestine to Jewish immigration, Holocaust survivors could not go there easily. They settled in the D.P. camps within the U.S. and British zones of occupation in Germany.

There was no employment available in the camps. There was barely sufficient food and clothing, and the camps provided only a temporary refuge. While Holocaust survivors in D.P. camps sought other possible alternatives, two thirds of the 300,000 Jews in D.P camps choose to go to Palestine (Bauer, 1982). During the later months of 1945 and in 1946, the organized efforts of the Bricha, the Jewish Brigade, and the Aliyah Beth all aided survivors to get to Israel. These organizations were defined as "illegal" by the British forces who controlled that area of Germany. Among survivors of the Holocaust, there were those who sought to immigrate to Israel to establish new lives there because of idealistic reasons e.g., live in their homeland, experience the spirituality of Israel and because of their Holocaust experiences. The following replies by our respondents provide examples of how their experiences during the Holocaust and in the aftermath, brought them to the decision to seek Aliyah (immigration) to Israel:

"Anti-Semitism in Europe and memories from the camps";

"Because of anti-Semitism. Everyone went to Israel, and we went as well";

"I wanted to escape from anti-Semitism";

"In Poland not many Jews were left and there was anti-Semitism. The Poles and the Russians blamed us for helping the Nazis kill Jews. The situation was intolerable, therefore we decided to immigrate to Israel";

"Anti-Semitism was increasing. I was wishing to join other members of my family that were already in Israel";

"I could not stay any more in Romania. I went to Israel 'illegally' with the Hashomer Hatzayeer movement";

"I did not want to stay in Europe in which the conditions were tough in every place. The gentiles were robbing our property";

"Not to live among the gentiles who were anti-Semites";

"After the war I did return to the village, but there was not anything to look for, I was waiting for a certain period and I immigrated to Israel";

"There was no reason to remain in Hungary. With the help of the "Hashomer Hatzayeer" we crossed to Austria and to Italy. From there, in an illegal way with the 'Maapeelim' ship, we immigrated to Israel on 3/8/1948";

"I was escaping from the country in which I was living. I wanted to leave it as quickly as possible after the Holocaust, to go to a safer land. So, at least, it seemed to me that Palestine would be safer for the Jews";

"After the Holocaust I wanted, all the time, only to immigrate to Israel, in order that we will have a state of our own. Therefore, I did not want to consider going to other countries but only to Israel";

"In 1946 I immigrated to Israel after I reached the conclusion that after the Holocaust we needed a country of our own";

"After the difficult period, I felt a strong need to immigrate to Israel with my family, which included my mother and my two sisters";

"The Holocaust made me more aware of the idea that there cannot be a nation without a state. I was thinking that the place of the Jewish nation is in Israel. And it is obvious that in Israel I feel the most protected"

"To establish a home. That what happened to my parents will not happen to me. That I will be a type A person and not a passive type B one";

"As I said, the reasons for my immigration to Israel derived from the conclusion that the only place for Jews is Israel. I arrived at this conclusion because of all that happened to me and because of an intense conviction to immigrate to Israel";

"I did not want to live in the Diaspora any more. Every place that I was walking on it, I knew that Jewish blood was spilled there. I was restless, I was afraid that the nightmare is not over yet";

"We didn't want to live in a place in which they murdered Jews, and this is the main reason that we turned out to be Zionists";

"My full recognition of the fact that after all what happened in the Holocaust, the conclusion is that there is not any other way but to live in Israel. Every nation has to live in its country. Therefore, I am here (in Israel), although there are many attractions to travel to other countries";

In summarizing respondents' views, a significant number of participants in our research indicated that Zionism and the love for Israel was the major motivating force for their wanting to immigrate to Israel at the end of the war. Others expressed matter of fact statements that Israel was the place they wanted to go to; some stated that they wanted to establish a Jewish state there and or that they wanted to live with other Jews in a country of their own given their persecution in Europe:

"I was a Zionist and I wanted to immigrate to Israel";

"I was a Zionist, and I wanted to live in my own country";

"I got quite a Zionist education at home and that is why I came to the decision that Israel is my country";

"I was a member of a national religious party, which believed in Zionism";

"The reasons that I immigrated were Zionist religious reasons";

"A Zionist education that I was absorbing in my home from the moment I was born";
"I was a Zionist. I was educated in the "Hashomer Hatzayeer;"

"I was a Zionist. This was the education, which I got at my parents' house";

"I was a Zionist, and although I found satisfaction and pleasure in my life in France, I felt that my life would not be fulfilled if I would not be immigrating to Israel";

"My background; Zionist activity in a Zionist movement. Worrying about the future, the children, I viewed problems, then, from security point of view";

"Since I was a member at the Zionist organization-I wanted to be independent and to make Aliyah and to study to be a nurse in Israel";

"I joined the Beitar youth movement. Then, I Joined Etzel (Irgun Tzevayi Leumi, headed by Begin) and this was how we got to come with Altelena (a ship organized by Beitar). I joined the Zionist youth movement, hoping to settle in Israel. My parents started to take care of their immigration to Israel. In 1948 we got settled in Israel";

"My husband was a Zionist and convinced me for several years to make Aliyah. And finally I was convinced and we made Aliyah together";

"I was in a kibbutz P'AGI (Poaley Agudat Israel), and representatives from Israel came to that place, and took care to transfer us on the ship "Negba" to Israel";

"We were together in the Hachshara preparing for Aliyah to Israel. Our entire kibbutz immigrated to Israel in a legal way in year 1949, on the "Independence.""

"We were thinking all the years that we should go to Israel. I wanted to live in Israel; In 1949 I immigrated to Israel. I wanted to be with Jews in my own country";

I always wanted to make Aliyah to Israel. I was left with one brother only, and both of us wanted to be together in our land;

"I always was hoping to immigrate to Israel, and in 1951 my husband and I decided that it was the right time";

"We knew that only in Israel we will be able to live among Jews, and we went for it. We waited three years in Italy and when the first cease fire started, we immigrated with the help of the "Mossad" on the legal ship "Kedma". My husband was already drafted in Italy to serve in the Israeli Army";

"I was hoping to establish together with my husband our home in Israel. I decided that in Israel it was the best. As a matter of fact, already before the war there was such an intention. My husband returned to his work after the war. My children immigrated first, and I immigrated after my husband passed away";

"I was a pioneer. And my main objective was to immigrate to Israel; I was thinking that my place was in Israel";

"This was a goal from childhood and the education of my parents towards this direction helped us get there. After the war our strongest will was to immigrate to Israel"

Whereas the above statements indicate that a majority of our respondents indicated ideological and Zionist motives, a small but significant group stated a more conventional reason as their motivation for immigrating to Israel. They wanted to join family members who were living in Israel, or that life circumstances got them to settle in Israel, without any strong interest or commitment to get there. The following examples are illustrative of this group:

"All the family was in Israel. There was not one relative in Poland, only in Israel there was an uncle. Later, I became a Zionist";

"My brother arrived in Israel and I wanted to be with him. I decided that to settle in England by myself, does not make sense. I did not consider England as a place to settle in permanently";

"I had in Israel a family and there I was by myself with my daughter. I waited 6 years to get permission to immigrate. We went through Austria";

"I did not have anyone in Czechoslovakia and I knew that I had a sister in Israel. I wanted to immigrate to our holy land, to get out from the Diaspora and to be with my parents";

"There was nowhere else to go. We emigrated from Germany with the help of the Jewish Agency. We got documents and immigrated to Israel legally";

"With a ship. My brother-in-law arranged the papers for me. A general tendency of the Jews at that time. I did not have what to lose";

"Aliyah B in 1947. I was expelled to Cyprus. And with the establishment of the State of Israel I returned and I was immediately recruited to the army";

"From Poland (through Italy) we immigrated to Israel on the ship "Moledet". The British discovered us in mid sea and they transferred us to Cyprus for two years. There I got married and my first son was born";

"I was staying in a refugee camp in Germany and from there I was transferred to Israel by the Agency. I arrived at Haifa's port and the British sent me to Cyprus. From there, using the papers of a young girl 16 years old, I was sent to Israel. In reality, I was already married and much older";

"Tito gave permission, and in the first ship, which went from Yugoslavia, from Trieste, I sailed directly to Israel. The JOINT helped with the expenditures";

"Illegal Aliyah from Marseilles in France, with a group of friends. We arrived at an immigrants' camp in Benyameena. I moved to live with relatives and, afterwards, to Beth Hachalutzot (Home of the Pioneer Women) in Tel-Aviv",

"At the end of the war I was in a transition camp in Italy. From there, we came in a boat which was in bad conditions, I don't remember its name";

"1946-48, we were waiting to immigrate to Israel, till we went as registered for a kibbutz".

"From the camp of displaced people in Germany, we immigrated to Israel by the Jewish Agency on the ship "Pan-York" in 1948";

There are some significant differences between those who chose the U.S. as their destination and those who wanted to settle in Palestine. Those who came to the U.S. were more likely to have family connections at that time who aided them with the application procedures, sent them affidavits and, in some instances, paid for the travel costs. Additionally, those seeking to go to the U.S. did so because they thought of the U.S. as a land of opportunity for personal freedom and for pursuit of economic achievements. Those who went to Israel were more likely to do so because of a Zionist orientation and/or background and because of personal convictions. They arrived in Israel after their Holocaust experiences, to contribute to the establishment of a Jewish state. They were aware of the difficulties they were likely to face there and were willing to relate to the challenges, which awaited them upon arrival.

OTHER DESTINATIONS

For those who did not go directly to Israel or to the U.S., the choice concerning a country of destination was more complicated. Other countries mentioned by our respondents (in order of frequency of response) were England, France, Canada, Sweden, Belgium, China, and Australia. The reasons given for choosing a particular country were diverse. For those more fortunate, friends and relatives made connections. For the remainder, fate or opportunity brought them there. Those who chose countries other than the U.S. or Israel did so either because of personal ties there or because that was seen as the only alternative. All these were interim destinations for our respondents who arrived, eventually, either to the U.S. or to Israel.

France was chosen initially by some survivors as a place to settle in, for its close proximity to Germany and "as an interlude" of peace and stability before moving on. Some noted that they had relatives or job opportunities, while others were just hoping to escape communist regimes (those who arrived from Poland, Hungary and Czechoslovakia).

England and Canada were countries chosen by some survivors more by default than by design. One immigrant to England stated that, "It was my only opportunity to leave Germany. I tried Israel and the U.S., but it took too long," The same was true for Canada; where one respondents said: "I was gravely ill after the Hungarian Revolution and when I could travel, the doors to the U.S. were closed. I could go to Canada,"

Those who initially went to Sweden usually had health problems and were sent there by the Red Cross immediately at the end of the war. One respondent stayed in Sweden because "country and people were good to us. Also, it was all we knew," Poland wasn't the type of country that survivors could or wanted to stay in. Those who were there felt trapped or were awaiting a U.S. visa: "It (Poland) was communistic, with no opportunity to leave."

China was an alternative destination for some survivors because "it was the only place open that you could go to without an affidavit," Only one respondent mentioned Australia. He had friends there.

CHALLENGES AND OPPORTUNITIES IN THE NEW LANDS

This section reviews difficulties in gaining access to the U.S. and Palestine for Jewish Holocaust survivors, and the challenges and opportunities, which awaited them upon their arrival. There were significant differences in the immigration experiences of Holocaust survivors and in the challenges, which they faced both in the U.S. and in Israel.

Neither the U.S. nor Palestine was accessible for immigration to Jews shortly before World War II during the war years, or in the immediate aftermath. Entry into the U.S. was possible only on the basis of immigration quotas allotted to European countries. There were no special opportunities for Jews, who were often discriminated against by immigration officials. Efforts to get Jews who escaped from Europe into the U.S. failed, and those who arrived :"illegally" to its shores were turned away. In the aftermath of WWII, the U.S. leadership participated in various international and Anglo-American commissions to solve the problems of displaced persons, generally including those of Jewish Holocaust survivors. The resolutions sought by the U.S. were directed toward allowing increased immigration quotas for Jewish Holocaust survivors into Palestine and, later, the partition of Palestine into Jewish and Arab sections by the United Nations. (Bauer, 1982). It was not until 1948, when the first Displaced Persons Act was passed by the U.S. Congress, that there was special consideration for the European refugees. Both the 1948 and 1950 Displaced Persons Acts reflected an American concern for the D.P.'s. However most of those who were eligible to enter the U.S. under these acts were not Jews. Indeed some Jewish leaders characterized the 1948 D.P. Act as a bill to exclude Jewish D.P.'s and to admit Hitler's collaborators. Only after lengthy efforts and after most Jewish D.P.'s had gone to Israel, did the U.S. Congress eliminate some of the provisions which excluded Jewish war refugees. In general, then, entry of Jews into the U.S. faced a multitude of legislative and bureaucratic obstacles. Many survivors waited lengthy periods of time, some up to five years, until they received their entry visas and were allowed to immigrate to the U.S.

Until 1948, when the State of Israel was established, Palestine was not only closed to new immigrants but also full of obstacles to those who managed to get there. There was the opposition from the Arab population, the likelihood of an armed conflict, and a very uncertain future. The British government did everything in its power to close Palestine to Jewish immigration. The U.S. leadership, including President Truman, requested that the British permit 100, 000 Jewish D.P.'s to enter Palestine in September 1945. The British concluded, that in light of their tenuous status in the Middle East at that time, they did not want to take any pro-Jewish stand. In 1946, a joint Anglo-American Committee of Inquiry concluded that entry of 100,000 Jews to Palestine was a logical and positive step (Bauer, 1982).

The British government continued to place various obstacles to immigration. In 1946, the British started to ship "illegal" immigrants to Cyprus. Some 50,000 persons spent up to two years in detention camps there until the establishment of the State of Israel, when they were allowed to arrive in Israel. There were ongoing deliberations at the Anglo-American and international levels concerning Jewish immigration to Palestine, the termination of the British mandate, and the partition of Palestine into Jewish and Arab states. While these deliberations were taking place, restriction on Jewish immigration to Palestine continued. During these years, the "illegal" immigration department of the Haganah took matters into its own hands by arranging the purchase of ships, the transport of immigrants "illegally" to Palestine, and their absorption there. In spite of the British restrictions, "illegal" immigration brought to Palestine approximately 70,000 Holocaust survivors from D.P. camps in Europe between 1945 and 1948.

There were some marked differences in the experiences awaiting the arrival of survivors to the U.S. and Palestine. Survivors who arrived in the U.S. faced the challenges of adaptation to a new environment, which was very different from the countries of their origin. The challenges, which they faced, entailed establishing an economic base of security for themselves and for their dependents, and to establish themselves in their new communities. Those who had established occupations had no difficulty finding employment. Others acquired training, and a few pursued degrees in higher education. According to various accounts, the majority of survivors managed in a relatively short period of time, to become constructive tax paying members of their respective communities. They established families and went about evolving for themselves a network of social relationships. The areas in which they experienced considerable difficulty were those of acculturation to the American Jewish community and to the general American community. In the years immediately following World War II pressures were exerted on newly arriving immigrants to adjust to the opportunities afforded by the "melting pot," i.e., give up their old-world ways and become integrated into the surrounding Jewish and general American communities. For many survivors this posed a special conflict. Some Holocaust survivors viewed their survival as entrusting upon them an imperative to continue and perpetuate that which Hitler wanted to destroy; Jewish life and culture. Therefore, they did not join established synagogues but established their own and went about in various ways to perpetuate traditional old-world Jewish life styles. They also went about and established Holocaust commemoration symbols and activities. Only in more recent decades has there been a general acceptance of the concept of the culturally pluralistic society. The consequence of the more recent respect for diversity, also drew respect for the life styles and traditions which were embodied by Holocaust survivors.

In Israel, the challenges awaiting survivors of the Holocaust were of a different nature. The Jewish population was subjected to a crisis involving hostilities from the Arab populations as well as from representatives of the British government. The years of 1946 through 1949 were characterized by a struggle for the establishment of the State of Israel. A significant number of younger Holocaust survivors took part in the pre-war military activities and in the War of Independence. This enabled many survivors to have the sense that they have actually contributed to the establishment of the State of Israel. While the State of Israel can not be seen as resulting directly from the Holocaust, the pressures of the Holocaust experience, the presence of Holocaust survivors in D.P. camps, and the arrival of Holocaust survivors to Israel decisively influenced the establishment of the State of Israel (Bauer, 1982; Sachar, 1987).

Survivors faced hardships and difficult economic challenges in Israel. The period of 1948 through 1952 saw tremendous expansion of the Jewish population in the State of Israel. The hardships included shortages and the rationing of food, faced by all. These hardships, along with continued hostilities from neighboring Arab countries brought about an outbound flow of Jewish population primarily toward the U.S. Survivors also faced a serious cultural challenge in Israel. As in the U.S., the prevailing norm was one that favored abandoning the 'faulty ways' and traditions of the Diaspora and, instead, the development of a new breed of Israeli who could actively defend the integrity of the Jewish state. While many Holocaust survivors took part in the establishment of the State of Israel, they were not ready to abandon their cultural heritage and the life styles which they wanted to perpetuate. Again, it was not until the State of Israel went through the maturation process that the commemoration of the Holocaust became incorporated into the symbolic and cultural traditions of Israel. Yad Vashem, a National Holocaust Memorial Museum was established in Jerusalem and the Yom Hashoah day was designated to honor the memory of Holocaust victims and remembrance of the historical events that characterized the Holocaust.

REFERENCES

Bauer, Y. (1982). *A History of the Holocaust*. New York: Franklin Watts.

Dinnerstein, L. (1982). *America and the Survivors of the Holocaust*. New York: Columbia University Press.

Harel, Z., Biegel, D.E., Gutmann, D (1994). *Jewish Aged in the United States and Israel: Diversity, Programs, and Services*. New York: Springer.

Helmreich, W. (1990). The impact of Holocaust survivors on American Society: A sociocultural portrait. In J. Gurock (Ed.), *American Jewish Life 1920–1990* (pp. 61–74). New York: Routledge.

Hilberg, R. (1985). *The Destruction of European Jews*. New York: Holmes & Meier.

Kahana, B. Harel, Z. & Kahana, E. (1988). Predictors of Psychological Well-Being Among Survivors of the Holocaust. In John P. Wilson, Zev Harel and Boaz Kahana (Eds.). *Human Adaptation to Extreme Stress: From the Holocaust to Vietnam*, (p. 171–192). New York: Plenum Press.

Lookstein, H. (1985) Were We Our Brothers' Keepers? New York: Hartmore House.

Nachmani, A. (1986). *Great Power Discord in Palestine*. London: Frank Cass.

Sachar, H.M. (1987). *A History of Israel*. New York: Oxford University Press.

Wyman, D. (1984). *The Abandonment of the Jews*. New York: Pantheon Books.

4

Cumulative Stress Experiences of Holocaust Survivors and the Immigrant Comparison Group

Our study on the impact of the Holocaust on survivors' lives has been anchored in the broader stress paradigm (Pearlin, 1989; Dohrenwend, 1998; Wheaton, 1994). Researchers in this burgeoning field have increasingly recognized the importance of aggregating life long stressors, which may involve phenomena ranging from daily hassles to severe trauma. Even as we focus on the aftermath of one of the most extreme forms of adversity known to man, we are interested in taking a more detailed look at life long stress experiences of survivors and members of the comparison group. Additionally, we consider the role of recent life events (Krause, 1991) in contributing to cumulative stress endured by our respondents.

Following up on our prior work on transactional stress models (Kahana, Redmond, Hill, Kahana, & Kercher, 1995), we consider stress in a multidimensional framework. Thus, we consider both enduring and immediate stress contexts, both past and present stressors and both chronic stress and discrete stressful experiences (Kahana, Kahana, Harel, Kelly, Monaghan, & Holland, 1997).

Garwood (1996) suggests that the four major elements of trauma suffered by Holocaust survivors are powerlessness, fear of annihilation, object loss, and torture. In addition to the original trauma suffered during the Holocaust, long-term survivors are also confronted with chronic stressors residual to the psychological isolation, and stigma (Kahana et al, 1997). Furthermore, survivors, like others, also confront normative chronic life stresses, along with the possibility of non-normative, post-Holocaust trauma, such as the Gulf War Scud missile attacks on Israel (Solomon & Prager,

1992). Understanding the long-term effect of the original trauma involves an appreciation of such cumulative life stresses.

LIFE CRISES

In our comparisons between survivors of the Holocaust and older adults who were prewar immigrants, we recognize that the absence or presence of the overwhelming trauma of the Holocaust differentiates the lives of the two groups. At the same time, in any comprehensive study of stress exposure, we must recognize that a broad spectrum of personal life crises experienced throughout life may also differentiate the lives of any two individuals. In this chapter, we take a more textured look at life crises experienced by survivors and immigrants using the Antonovsky Life Crisis Inventory (1974).

In making comparisons focusing on stress exposure throughout life, we recognize that life crises reported would include both Holocaust related and general life stressors. Since the Life Crisis Inventory includes life long trauma, we anticipate that Holocaust survivors would report significantly greater incidence of diverse life crises. Furthermore, it would enrich our understanding if we can compare survivors with immigrants and place both groups' life crisis exposure in the context of typical U.S. born elderly who were not exposed either to the Holocaust or to the crises posed by escaping one's previous homeland due to impending war and persecution.

We recognize that past traumatic events or life crises, even extending as far back as childhood, can have an adverse effect on late life well being (Kahana, 1992). Past traumas may also adversely affect ability to cope with future stress, leading to greater vulnerability in late life (Wheaton, 1994).

The Antonovsky Life Crisis Inventory (Antonovsky, 1974) ascertains the occurrence of a number of major personal stressors that may occur through-out life. Items include severe threats to life such as insufficient food, wartime depravations, the experience of life threatening illness. They also include severe interpersonal stressors such as constant quarrelling with a significant other; having been betrayed by a significant other, or experiencing enduring tension. Family related stressors include bad home situation; having grown up without parents; the loss of a partner through divorce or widowhood. Work related negative experiences are also considered, such as not being able to find a job, job loss, forced job change, being denied promotion, and having trouble with a co-worker.

Since life crises are generally viewed as independent of one another, items are considered individually and summated as an index. Results of comparisons in life crises endured between survivors and immigrants are shown in Table 1.

Table 1. Antonovsky's Life Crises History

	Survivors	Immigrants	
Personal Challenges	%	%	p
Not enough food			
USA	20.7	7.7	.001
Israel	20.7	14.2	.12
Life endangering illness			
USA	64.4	30.2	.001
Israel	43.3	26.5	.001
Quarreled with a significant other			
USA	14.6	3.3	.001
Israel	18.7	14.1	.26
Betrayed by trusted other			
USA	38.4	13.0	.001
Israel	22.7	17.5	.25
Too many responsibilities			
USA	38.0	16.3	.001
Israel	16.5	14.9	.70
High tension			
USA	65.8	73.5	.14
Israel	43.2	37.0	.31
No way out of debt			
USA	16.3	4.0	.001
Israel	13.3	11.7	.65
Bad home situation			
USA	21.7	6.5	.001
Israel	16.0	7.6	.02
Not living with parents when a child			
USA	22.1	16.1	.18
Israel	29.3	18.1	.02
Divorce/widowhood			
USA	33.1	40.9	.15
Israel	28.6	29.0	.94
Employment Related Life Crises			
Not able to find work			
USA	39.4	22.6	.001
Israel	23.3	21.9	.76
Job change			
USA	29.5	33.8	.42
Israel	20.5	29.9	.05
Lost job			
USA	26.1	35.8	.06
Israel	17.4	12.7	.23
Denied promotion			
USA	7.8	11.3	.31
Israel	15.3	13.1	.56
Difficulty with fellow worker			
USA	17.4	11.9	.17
Israel	14.2	14.1	.97

(*Cont.*)

Table 1. (*Cont.*)

	Survivors	Immigrants	
Personal Losses and war time experiences	%	%	p
Death of sibling			
USA	19.8	6.7	.001
Israel	17.7	17.3	.93
Death of child			
USA	19.9	12.2	.07
Israel	11.8	14.2	.52
Bad wartime experiences			
USA	98.2	36.4	.001
Israel	79.3	27.8	.001
Fight in war			
USA	16.5	7.8	.02
Israel	19.1	18.3	.85

Overall, our results reveal that survivors experienced significantly greater incidence of most major life crises, particularly in areas which may be related to deprivations of war. In terms of personal challenges, survivors living in the United States, experienced significantly more life crises than immigrants in areas of not having enough food to eat ($p < .001$), life endangering illnesses ($p < .001$), quarrelsome situations with a significant other ($p < .001$); having been betrayed by a significant other ($p < .001$), having been burdened by too many responsibilities ($p < .001$), not having found a way out of debt ($p < .001$), and having experienced a bad home situation ($p < .001$). Only in terms of two interpersonal areas, living in high tension environments and divorce or widowhood, did immigrants and survivors in the U.S. report similar experiences.

Survivors in Israel also reported more personal stressors than did immigrant respondents there. Only on three of these stressors, however, were the differences significant: life endangering illnesses ($p < .001$), bad home situation ($p < .02$), and not having grown up living with both parents ($p < .02$). On employment related stressors there were limited differences between Holocaust survivors in the United States and Israel. In the United States, survivors, compared with immigrant respondents, had significantly ($p < .001$) greater difficulty getting their first job. Once working, however, survivors were slightly, but not significantly, less likely to change jobs or lose their jobs. In Israel the only significant difference reported was in job change ($p = .05$), with immigrants reporting more frequent job changes.

Survivors, compared with immigrants, in the United States were significantly more likely to have lost a brother or sister to death ($p < .001$) or lost a child to death ($p < .07$). No differences were found on these losses in Israel. Survivors, as expected, reported considerably more ($p < .001$) bad wartime experiences in both countries. Similarly, survivors in the United States reported a significantly higher number of incidents ($p < .02$) of participation and fighting in a war than did immigrants. In Israel, there were no such differences reported as a significant number of Holocaust survivors enlisted in the Israel Defense Forces and participated in the various wars.

In addition to considering comparisons between survivors and immigrants in experiencing life crises and recent life events, it is noteworthy that we can also compare these two populations with U.S. born elderly persons whom we have studied in a different context. We have comparable data on selected Antonovsky life crises and recent life events for 419 residents of Florida retirement communities (Kahana & Kahana, 2003). It is notable that smaller percentages of U.S. born retirees report having experienced life crises than either Holocaust survivors or immigrants. It is particularly interesting that even in the area of work-related crises, the U.S. group experienced far fewer stressors than either Holocaust survivors or immigrants. While our comparisons of survivors and immigrants tend to highlight that survivors endured many more life crises than did the immigrant group, our opportunity to make comparisons with U.S. born populations calls attention to the fact that our immigrants also represent a group who have endured excessive life crises. Most of these individuals were uprooted from their homeland due to the imminent threat of the Holocaust, endured job and personal discrimination, and also had to cope with immigration related stress.

Survivors, as well as the prewar immigrants who constitute our comparison group, faced many obstacles as they attempted to establish themselves in a trade or profession, and aimed to earn a living in their adoptive countries. Additionally, many survivors experienced multiple relocations until they finally settled in a permanent home. Learning the language and culture of their new country introduced additional challenges. For many, these stressors resolved themselves as they adapted to their new homeland. For others, these stressors continued well into old age (Kahana, Harel, & Kahana, 1988). Chronic stressors of immigration include a broad array of challenges ranging from economic hardships to social marginality. Portes and Rumbaut (1996) suggest that one major source of immigration related stress is due to the surrendering of old roots before new ones can be established. For Holocaust survivors, surrendering of old roots was not a voluntary process, but occurred as a result of turmoil and instability. Acculturation can be traumatic because the immigrants are simultaneously distancing themselves from the culture in which they grew up and embracing a new and foreign one in its place. In the case of survivors of the Holocaust, this picture gets even more complex, since survivors are products of three different cultures. Thus, survivors may have been socialized during childhood into Hungarian or Polish culture in their country of origin, and subsequently immigrated to the U.S.

or Israel. In addition, for most, their basic ethnic identity is their Jewish religious, cultural, and ethnic heritage.

Since immigration was a challenge faced by, survivors and immigrants, we did not anticipate major differences in this area between respondent groups. Issues pertaining to learning a new language, obtaining work, and learning new customs were shared by both groups. Among open-ended responses of survivors about major problems faced after arrival to the U.S., 41% spontaneously cited language problems, 47% cited problems with finding work, and only 9% cited problems with getting used to customs in their new locale. Nevertheless, the added vulnerability of survivors based on the trauma they endured may have exacerbated the stress of being an immigrant.

In response to open-ended questions about post-war experiences and challenges, survivors' comments reflect the long-term stress of being immigrants and of being different. A woman, age 80, responded, "We started a new life in so many countries. It was too much. I love America, but it was too much starting new all the time." A man, age 72, reflected, "It changed a lot of things; I would be more respected if I was still home, here I am a little man, a plain person. Here you are not born, you don't have the language." A woman, age 70, stated, "Being with different kinds of people. It took me too long to adjust to this way of living. It's different. But I'm very happy to be here. I appreciate more everything I have. Here (in America) people take things for granted." Another survivor, now living in the U. S., noted, "I had a big future when I was young and I would have had a different kind of living, a better life, financially and emotionally feeling better. I wouldn't have been a painter."

RECENT LIFE EVENTS

Stress theories maintain that life events are stressful because they generate change. Negative events experienced by the elderly, in particular, frequently involve major life changes (e.g., death of a spouse). They include events of loss such as personal illness, illness of family members or friends, and interpersonal conflict that are often associated with subsequent depression or dysphoria (Pearlin & Mullan, 1992). Numerous studies show that experiencing undesirable or negative events tend to diminish subjective well being, even after controlling for other factors associated with mental health (Lin & Ensel, 1989; Okun, Melichar, & Hill, 1990).

Recent life event stress was assessed with the Recent Life Events Scale for Older Adults. This is a checklist of 17 events adapted by Kahana and associates (Kahana, Fairchild, & Kahana, 1982) for older respondents from the Schedule of Recent Life Events (Holmes & Rahe, 1967). Based on concerns about confounding of independent and dependent variables (French, Knox, & Gekoski, 1992; Kasl, 1992), items from the original scale assessing physical symptoms that are typically associated with mental health problems were not included in this inventory. Stressful events that were assessed include events in the lives of the respondents themselves and those that occurred in the lives of a child or family member. Specific events considered are listed in Table 2.

Table 2. Recent Life Events (Experienced in the Past Year)

	Survivors	Immigrants	
Personal Life Events	%	%	P
Marital problems			
USA	2.6	2.5	.97
Israel	3.8	3.2	.77
Change of residence			
USA	1.8	5.8	.06
Israel	3.8	8.9	.05
Financial difficulty			
USA	15.2	1.3	.01
Israel	10.9	12.0	.58
Retired voluntarily			
USA	4.2	4.1	.93
Israel	10.9	12.0	.74
Forced to retire or leave job			
USA	4.2	0.7	.04
Israel	4.4	4.4	.99
Out of town trip			
USA	78.2	87.1	.04
Israel	50.1	59.9	.09
Stopped driving			
USA	2.4	0.0	.06
Israel	4.6	3.3	.56
Someone moved in with you			
USA	4.9	1.9	.15
Israel	6.5	5.7	.75
Major property loss or destruction			
USA	5.5	0.0	.01
Israel	3.3	7.0	.12
Personal accident or injury			
USA	4.2	3.9	.87
Israel	4.9	5.7	.74
Victim of crime			
USA	8.0	3.3	.07
Israel	4.3	10.1	.04

(*Cont.*)

Table 2. (*Cont.*)

	Survivors	Immigrants	
Events in the Lives of Significant Others	%	%	P
Separation/divorce of child			
USA	3.7	4.9	.60
Israel	5.4	5.1	.88
Illness, injury to family member			
USA	14.3	21.8	.08
Israel	21.0	21.5	.91
Birth of grandchild			
USA	28.0	17.9	.04
Israel	29.3	28.2	.82
Anniversary, family celebration			
USA	40.6	33.5	.19
Israel	33.5	37.3	.46
Child, grandchild engaged, married			
USA	13.0	13.1	.98
Israel	6.6	12.0	.08
Trouble with child, grandchild			
USA	7.5	5.7	.54
Israel	9.3	6.3	.31

Findings indicate generally low rates of troublesome recent life events. There were very limited differences between survivors and immigrants, both in the U.S. and Israel, concerning the experiences of recent life events. Of the personal life events, immigrants had more changes of residence than did survivors in both countries. In the United States, survivors, compared with immigrants, reported significantly more financial difficulties ($p < .01$), more forced retirements ($p < .04$), more stoppage of driving ($p < .06$), more property damage or destruction ($p < .01$), and more victimization episodes ($p < .07$). There were higher incidences of events happening to significant others than personal events reported by all respondents. Some of these recent life events referred to potentially happy occasions such as birth of a grandchild or family celebration. The only significant difference in this area referred to birth of a grandchild, with 28% of U.S.-based survivors compared to 19% of immigrants reporting a birth. While we include in this descriptive report both positive and negative life events in our multivariate analyses (see Chapter 8), we consider only negative recent life events as reflecting stressors. In interpreting these findings, we must keep in mind that reporting life events also entails an important appraisal process. It is possible that survivors were more vigilant and were sensitized to report events such as victimization and property destruction. Such differential appraisals of stress should also be considered in the context of chronic stressors, which Holocaust survivors live with in the aftermath of their traumatic experiences.

CHRONIC STRESSORS DUE TO SURVIVORSHIP

The concept of chronic stress implies a temporally extended and lasting challenge to the individual. The specific trauma of the Holocaust, which occurred over fifty years ago, also requires a temporally anchored historical perspective. Accordingly, survivors of the Holocaust had experienced stress both during the period leading up to World War II, and subsequent to the Holocaust. These clusters of stressors were overshadowed by the enormity of the trauma endured during the Holocaust. Social functioning, psychological well-being, and adaptation to old age among these survivors are the consequences of complex interactions between the full array of traumatic stressors and general life stressors, which they experienced (Kahana, 1992).

Chronic stressors have been added relatively recently to the general stress paradigm to complement the stressors posed by acute life events (Kahana & Kahana, 1998). The major characteristics of chronic stressors are their enduring and ongoing (or long-term) nature (Wheaton, 1997). Victims of extreme stressors, such as the Holocaust, may have long-term intrusive memories of trauma and may be stigmatized because of their experiences. A distinguishing feature of their trauma is the strong probability that it will lead to long-term chronic stress. Trauma constitutes a constellation of environmental assaults, which have ripple effects in creating further enduring chronic stressors. Some of the chronic internalized stressors which continue to disrupt the lives of survivors (i.e., intrusive thoughts such as nightmares) are conceptualized in the trauma literature as outcomes reflecting PTSD. The present conceptualization describes the ways these intrusive symptoms can produce further stressful experiences.

Long-term survivors of trauma are expected to deal with clusters of stressors, which are temporally organized around the traumatic event. Independent of the traumatic events endured, they are also likely to face normative stressors throughout the life course. Most of the normative stress clusters are time-limited and are resolved after the period of time has elapsed. However, the greatest continuing challenge faced by survivors is posed by the stress cluster, which we term "chronic post-traumatic stressors". These are residual internalized stressors, which originate from the trauma and continue to afflict survivors on an indefinite basis (Tanay, 2004).

Our framework considers the spectrum of life crises and chronic stressors faced by elderly Holocaust survivors. Stressors clustered around the historical event of the trauma may be temporally classified as pre-traumatic stressors, traumatic stressors, and post-traumatic stressors. Normative stressors and crises of the life course may be categorized as childhood, adult, and old age related stressors. These two distinct though interrelated groups of stressors ultimately impinge on late life well-being of the elderly survivors. Here we review key characteristics of each of these clusters of stressors that we have described previously (Kahana, et al., 1997) and then turn to a more extended discussion of chronic post-traumatic stressors resulting from Holocaust trauma.

TRAUMA RELATED STRESSORS

1. Pre-War Stressors. In considering the chronic nature of the trauma of the Holocaust, it is important to note that there was an extended period of threat and discrimination endured by many survivors even prior to the escalation of persecution, which culminated in the Holocaust. In narratives of their life experiences, all respondents (including both survivors and refugees) often referred to periods of prewar stress when they were subjected to prejudice and discrimination. For instance, many respondents were unable to complete their education because of the policies restricting entry of Jewish students to universities. Economic discrimination against Jews, destruction of property, and threat to personal safety also characterized respondents' life experiences during this period.

2. Holocaust Traumatic Stressors. Holocaust traumatic stressors relate to the events of the trauma itself. The period of traumatization was a cataclysmic period for survivors of the Holocaust, in which acute and chronic stressors enveloped the survivor's very existence. Stresses of the Holocaust included "cumulative effects of prolonged physical abuse, degradation, hunger, exposure to unbearable weather, lethal labor, repeated losses, and above all, the constant threat of extermination and death—all in the absence of normative civilized laws and principles" (Lomrantz, 1990). Thus, the original trauma of the Holocaust may be described as chronic, based on its all encompassing quality and its duration.

Much of the voluminous literature on the Holocaust focuses on stressors of the original trauma (Berger, 2002; Krystal, 1968). It may be argued that the efforts marshaled by survivors to cope with this original trauma will largely determine the extent of their ultimate recovery from the trauma and their late life well-being. Our framework suggests that the original traumatization is the source of the trauma-related secondary stressors, and impacts on both appraisals and modes of coping in dealing with other chronic life stressors during the post-Holocaust period.

3. Post-War Stressors. Reports of Holocaust survivors in our study reveal that the immediate postwar period was also fraught with many acute and

chronic stressors, creating further trauma for survivors. Content analyses of our interviews with Holocaust survivors in the United States reveal a series of general postwar stressors, including the need to face perpetrators and bystanders, searching for relatives, and searching for a new country to call home. Post-war deprivations were reflected in illness and lack of food, clothing, and shelter. In addition, stressors unique to certain survivor groups included living in displaced persons (DP) camps, living under Communist persecution, or living in war-torn Israel. Chronic stressors also emerged as most survivors became refugees after the Holocaust and faced the challenges of establishing a new life in a new land.

4. Chronic Post-Traumatic Stressors. Chronic stressors, which are directly related to the trauma experienced during the Holocaust, represent the major focus of our discussion here. We identify these stressors as "chronic post-traumatic stressors" which are distinct outcomes of the original traumatic stress. The traumatic Holocaust event is now over and the threat of its recurrence is remote. Hence, the chronic stressors of Holocaust trauma may be viewed as residual stressors (both internal and external), left by the original trauma. For survivors of the Holocaust, there are four important post-traumatic stressors: intrusive memories of trauma, living with fear and mistrust, social and psychological isolation, and living with stigma. The first two represent internalized stressors reflected in cognitive or emotional states, whereas the third and fourth are primarily social stressors, with both internal and external components. We will turn to a more extensive discussion of each of these types of chronic stressors because they comprise the major focus of our post-traumatic chronic stress framework.

INTRUSIVE MEMORIES OF TRAUMA

Intrusive memories constitute a major class of chronic stressors for survivors of extreme trauma such as the Holocaust. These memories are ongoing internalized reminders of the trauma endured. It has been argued that such intrusive imagery is a major mechanism by which trauma translates into chronic distress (Baum, Cohen, & Hall, 1993). Persistent thoughts or recollections of such trauma have been reported among diverse traumatized populations, and have been found to be associated with distress and performance deficits. (Nolen-Hoeksema, Morrow, & Fredrickson, 1993). Based on a series of research projects focusing on war veterans and survivors of natural disaster, Baum (1990) indicates that the longer the time since the trauma, the more intrusive memories predict adverse psychological and physical health outcomes.

Intrusive memories cause survivors to continuously re-live traumatic experiences. Traumatic memories may be triggered by adverse and often unpredictable stimuli ranging from sensory experiences to anniversaries or media reports reminiscent of the type of trauma endured (McCann & Pearlman, 1990). There is extensive documentation in the field of traumatic stress studies that such memories of trauma persist. These memories are used as one of several criteria for establishing a diagnosis of Post-Traumatic Stress Disorder (PTSD) (DSM-IV-TR, 2002).

Our study provided an opportunity for a deeper exploration of the nature of memories among survivors. Among survivors in our study, 61% reported that they think daily or several times a week about the Holocaust even forty years after their original traumatic experiences. A smaller group, (typically ranging between 5% and 20%), reported experiencing other symptoms of psychological distress which could be viewed as being related to PTSD. Thus, our data reveal that intrusive memories of trauma are normative rather than exceptional occurrences, even among survivors who do not exhibit the other symptoms of PTSD. Survivors of the Holocaust in both the U.S. and Israel reported significantly more intrusive thoughts than the comparison group in response to a subscale we created based on the SCL-90 items (Derogatis, 1977). The intrusive memories subscale displays a Chronbach's alpha of .60 and included items such as having frightening thoughts and images.

Traumatic memories are likely to emerge as intrusive images, which disrupt the psychological and social functioning of the trauma survivor (Paivio, 1986). To explore this phenomenon we compared survivors' accounts of traumatic Holocaust experiences with accounts of non-traumatic events experienced by survivors. Memories of events related to the Holocaust were described in significantly more vivid terms, using more visual imagery, than memories of events, which occurred immediately prior or subsequent to the Holocaust (p < .01). These findings support suggestions by Baum (1990) that memories of trauma impose themselves on the mind and frequently enter into awareness as visual images. We also found that intrusive memories of trauma reported by Holocaust survivors are significantly correlated with poor morale as measured by the Lawton Morale Scale (Lawton, 1975). Thus, among survivors living in Israel, a correlation of −.59 (p < .001) was reported between intrusive memories and morale. Among survivors living in the U. S., the correlation was −.61 (p < .001).

Such experiences of chronic stress, through intrusive memories, are exemplified in the following remarks by some of our respondents. For instance, a 58-year-old man stated, "I think about it [Holocaust] when I have to throw out food, or in my dreams. I think about it quite often." Another man, aged 84, stated, "We are more depressed. Others have not had our experiences; they have no depressing thoughts." A 57-year-old woman survivor reported, "You can't wipe the memories away; I have a bad feeling, maybe not having done enough for my brother." A survivor who was a child during the Holocaust reflected, "I think that people who were not in the Holocaust are healthier people; they don't have these types of memories to cope with. Bad memories don't help your emotional mentality." Another survivor who spent much of the Holocaust in a German labor camp responded, "Can't wash away, in back of my mind the Holocaust, no matter how much fun I'm having or how much I'm enjoying myself." These comments illustrate both the persistence of intrusive memories of trauma and survivors' recognition that these memories contribute to their psychological distress long after the original trauma occurred.

FEAR AND MISTRUST

A second, enduring internalized stressor that is experienced by Holocaust survivors is the pervasive sense of victimization, which may cause them to mistrust strangers, those in authority, or even anyone different from themselves. Survivors may see dangers lurking in their environment and find it hard to distinguish possible mishaps from probable ones (Kahana, Kahana, Harel, & Rosner, 1988). The experience of uncontrollable and non-normative events during the Holocaust conditioned a view of living in an uncontrollable world and resulted in maintaining a vigilant posture toward all possible future adversity. Based on this continuing sense of vulnerability, the physical and social environment may be experienced as chronically threatening. This appraisal-based experience of chronic stress is consistent with the cognitive stress paradigm proposed by Lazarus and Folkman (1984).

To determine the degree to which fear and mistrust of the social environment represent a continuing problem for survivors, a five-item scale was generated using relevant items from the SCL 90. The mistrust subscale yielded a Chronbach's alpha of .62. Items include statements such as "Most people can't be trusted" or "Others watch or talk about you". Survivors in the United States reported significantly higher mean scores on the fear and mistrust scale than did members of their comparison group. In contrast, survivors living in Israel did not appear to experience greater fears and mistrust relative to their comparison group.

Additionally, we found mistrust to have a greater negative correlation with morale for U.S. than for Israeli survivors. Speculatively, these findings suggest that those survivors living as part of an ethnic majority in their own homeland are less likely to experience the fear and victimization, or to be negatively affected by it. This finding exemplifies the way contextual factors shape appraisals of threat. Although, citizens of Israel continue to live in a social and physical milieu where war and terrorism are rampant, Israeli society somehow offers survivors a psychologically safe and reassuring milieu (Solomon 1995).

Experiences of living with fear and mistrust were frequently depicted by our U.S. survivors as they described their aging and how they differ from others who did not experience the trauma of the Holocaust. Thus, 34% of survivors reported being afraid of many things as compared to 12% of those in the comparison group. Yet, it should be noted that 60% of survivors do not report these fears, thereby testifying to survivor resilience.

The following statements in response to attitudes about one's aging illustrate the chronic stress of living with fear and mistrust. A 69-year-old woman survivor responded, "I live an older life, worry more, live with fear—the dreams make you crazy." Another woman, aged 72, stated, "I am reserved about trusting people, we were betrayed many times." A 67-year-old woman reflected, "I am always afraid something happens to me because I worry so much of the time. I worry about my children's future because I would like to see more peace in the world, because all of a sudden anything can go wrong." Another woman, age 59, stated, "We are concerned about the family, always wondering. God knows what tomorrow will bring." Another respondent who arrived home one day to find the German SS officers had taken away her mother observed, "I get more frightened for my children that another war should come." It is noteworthy that these statements of fear and mistrust relate to society at large or to generalized others rather than to specific individuals. Also, they clearly reflect fear of a repetition of some great trauma akin to the Holocaust.

Survivors may not fully recognize or acknowledge the internalized aspects of chronic stressors posed by living with fear and mistrust, and cannot find a direct referent for their fears. Hence, they may not be able to marshall appropriate coping strategies. This pattern contrasts with their general awareness of the chronic stressors represented by intrusive memories, which result in more deliberate coping efforts involving disclosure.

SOCIAL AND PSYCHOLOGICAL ISOLATION

The Holocaust-related chronic stressors discussed thus far, including intrusive memories of trauma, and feelings of vulnerability to victimization, reflect the internalization of components of the original trauma. The survivor thus becomes both the object and the source of stress. In the case of the chronic stress of isolation, the stress has both internalized and external social environmental components. In fact, there are two distinct chronic stressors, one involving the absence of kin and actual social isolation, and the other the internalized or psychological sense of isolation. In terms of the former, survivors lost the majority of their families of orientation including parents, aunts, uncles, and siblings. Although most survivors endeavored to marry or remarry and reconstitute their families, the experience of being alone and bereft of family is a recurrent chronic stressor reported by survivors.

In addition to the absence of social supports and connectedness, social isolation also appears to be intertwined with a more internalized sense of psychological isolation which has also been noted by other Holocaust scholars. Survivors often report a sense of loneliness, which borders on desolation (Helmreich, 1992). Psychological isolation also includes the sense of not being understood and accepted, and of being set apart from others. Part of this feeling may be based on the perception that one's traumatic experiences set one apart (Kahana, 2001).

A four-item social and psychological isolation subscale was constructed using selected SCL-90 items such as: "feeling lonely when with others" and "never feeling close to others". The Chronbach's alpha for this scale is .61. Significant differences in reported feelings of isolation were found between survivors and the comparison group in both the United States and Israel. It is noteworthy that 41% of U.S. survivors in our study report feeling lonely a lot, whereas only 22% of the comparison group indicates experiencing frequent loneliness.

Feelings of social and psychological isolation are exemplified by the following comments made by our study respondents. A 68 year-old woman survivor stated, "I'm envious of everybody who has a nice, good, big family. We have only one son and he lives in California—I had such a beautiful family before the war. We don't have a big family, and we are lonely." A 63-year-old man felt, "There is a missing link some place, I can't describe it. I'm missing my family. It's on my mind all the time." Another woman survivor, age 69, who had lost her mother and father and all of her eleven siblings during the Holocaust stated, "I always think of home, I get nostalgic feelings— I miss the closeness from my family. A lot of times I feel nobody knows me." These statements reveal the interconnected experiences of enduring social and psychological isolation among survivors of the Holocaust living in the United States. It is noteworthy that these feelings even applied to their families of procreation.

STIGMA

The clinical and scientific literature on survivors of the Holocaust convincingly demonstrates the intensely felt stigma associated with survivorship (Solomon, 1995). Survivors are widely depicted as "damaged goods" or persons whose suffering has irreparably affected their psychological well-being and social functioning (Kahana, Harel, & Kahana, 1988). The very propensity of clinicians to define traumatization based on the likelihood of developing PTSD suggests that those individuals who endured victimization will receive a psychiatric diagnosis (Green, 1993). Furthermore, the psychiatric illness label constitutes an additional chronic stressor (Goffman, 1963).

During the first three decades following the Holocaust, professionals painted a bleak picture of survivors, and the public at large turned a deaf ear to their experiences. In response to accounts of atrocities during the Holocaust, Americans often drew parallels to the Great Depression and admonished survivors not to feel sorry for themselves. In Israel there was also negative labeling of survivors (Solomon, 1995). It was often suggested that the survivors' inability to fight back may have contributed to their fate (Hass, 1995). The tendency of the larger society to trivialize the horrendous experiences of survivors resulted in survivors being deprived of the opportunity to communicate about their experiences. In this sense, social stigma placed constraints on the coping repertoire of survivors.

In order to ascertain whether living with stigma is recognized as a special problem by Holocaust survivors, a Living with Stigma Subscale was developed on the basis of four relevant SCL 90 items. The scale included statements such as "Others do not understand me or are unsympathetic" and "Others do not share my ideas and beliefs". The Chronbach's alpha was .61 for this subscale. Our findings follow the pattern observed for other chronic stressors, with significantly greater stigmatization reported by United States survivors than the U.S. comparison group. Furthermore, on each of the above items, the survivors differed significantly from the comparison group. No significant differences were observed between the two Israeli samples. It should be noted that rates of reported stigmatization were very low for all groups. In response to open-ended questions, survivors in our sample did not spontaneously refer to their stigmatized status. Nevertheless, some expressions of concern about the survivor label were noted. This is exemplified by one survivor, age 72, who stated, "I don't want to be labeled as a survivor."

Our data illustrate the fact that survivors show significantly greater concern about health, safety, and well-being of their offspring than do members of the comparison group. Such excessive fears about children's welfare represent chronic stressors for survivors in both the U.S. and Israel. Within the U.S., fully twice as many survivors (53%) as members of the comparison group (26%) stated that they worry about their children's driving safety (p < .001). Significant differences were also found among Israeli samples; 49% of survivors report excessive worrying versus 38% of the Israeli comparison group. Almost identical patterns of differences were obtained in considering worrying about children's physical health. Interestingly, in spite of fewer dangers facing adult children in the U.S., concern was more prevalent among survivors in the U.S. than in Israel. These findings fit with Aldwin's (1992) observations about the salience of "non-egocentric stressors" which are stressors experienced by significant others that assume greater importance as part of the generativity needs of older persons. One elderly survivor went as far as giving her two teenage grandchildren several quarters so that when they go out for the evening, they could call her 2 or 3 times until they got home, to let her know that they were safe.

It has been documented (Helmreich, 1992) that medical symptoms are particularly threatening to survivors of the Holocaust because concentration camp inmates who became ill or exhibited any symptoms of ill health during the Holocaust were put to death. Furthermore, mistrust of the medical establishment and medical regimes have also been found to characterize survivors (Krystal, 1968). Survivors in our study gave voice to these threatening appraisals of the chronic stress of ill health. A 68-year-old man stated, "I was never ill in my life before. I've had serious illness. It affected my heart. I don't know how [it affected me] mentally. I'm pretty sore. It affected my arthritis... sleeping naked on a cement floor, to be outside, not to be able to sit down, being punished."

We presented a framework for classifying chronic stressors, which impinge on older individuals who have experienced major trauma earlier in their lives, focusing on elderly survivors of the Holocaust. In our discussion, we have illustrated the multidimensional nature of the chronic stressors, which impinge on such survivors, and we have placed groups of stressors in a temporal context.

Surviving major trauma has a powerful influence on the subsequent chronic stressors to which survivors are exposed. It also impacts on their appraisals of normative or more general life stressors.

It should be noted that acute stressors, chronic stressors, coping efforts, and outcomes of distress versus recovery are difficult to separate. Nevertheless, focusing on the role of chronic stressors in the broader context of the traumatic stress framework should clarify components of the complex process of human adaptation to trauma (Hass, 1995). An important challenge in developing this paradigm relates to integrating the chronic stressors, which we focus on here, with discrete or acute stressors in a comprehensive model.

Furthermore, the nature of positive outcomes of coping with chronic stressors should be addressed (Lomranz, 1990). Is successful coping with trauma-related chronic stressors manifested in positive psychological well-being or in other important social outcomes? In the case of internalized trauma-related stressors, it may be argued that diminishing the stress or eliminating it is the ultimate desirable outcome. Thus, the goal of enhancing coping skills of survivors of trauma may be to help them learn to trust others, and to diminish the frequency and intensity of intrusive memories of trauma (McCann & Pearlman, 1990).

According to Raphael (1986), regardless of premorbid states, it is the reaction to severe trauma and the ability to integrate the traumatic experience that account for ultimate outcomes. Similarly, Rosenbloom

(1985) comments on the need to identify those adaptive and interpretive forces that assisted survivors in their rebirth and social integration. The ultimate challenge to survivors is to maintain or restore ego-integrity in later life by learning to trust again and to accept the entirety of their lives in spite of their horrendous life experiences.

REFERENCES

Aldwin, C.M. (1994). *Stress, Coping, and Development: An Integrative Perspective.* New York: Guilford Press.

American Psychological Association. (2002). Diagnostic and Statistical Manual of Mental Disorders, 4th Edition. Arlington VA: APA.

Antonovsky, A. (1974). Conceptual and Methodological Problems in the Study of Resistance Resources and Stressful Life Events. In B. Dohrenwend & B. Dohrenwend (Eds.). *Stressful Life Events: Their Nature and Effects* (pp. 245–258). New York: Wiley.

Baum, A. (1990). Stress, intrusive imagery, and chronic distress. *Health Psychology,* 9, 653–675.

Baum, A., Cohen, L., & Hall, M. (1993). Control and intrusive memories as possible determinants of chronic stress. *Psychosomatic Medicine,* 55(3), 274–286.

Berger, R. (2002). Fathoming the Holocaust: A Social Problems Approach. New York: Aldine de Gruyter.

Derogatis, L. & Cleary, P. (1977). Confirmation of the dimensional structure of the SCL-90: A study in construct validation, *Journal of Clinical Psychology,* 33(4), 981–989.

Dohrenwend, B.P., Ed. (1998). *Adversity, Stress and Psychopathology.* New York: Oxford University Press.

French, S.L., Knox, V.J., & Gekoski, W.L. (1992). Confounding as a problem in relating life events to health status in elderly individuals. *American Journal of Community Psychology,* 20(2), 243–252.

Garwood, A. (1996). The Holocaust and the power of powerlessness: Survivor guilt, an unhealed wound. *British Journal of Psychotherapy,* 13(2), 243–258.

Goffman, E. (1963). *Stigma: Notes on the Management of Spoiled Identity.* New York, NY: Simon and Schuster, Inc.

Green, B. (1993). Identifying Survivors at Risk: Trauma and Stressors Across Events. In J. P. Wilson & B. Raphael (Eds.), *International Handbook of Traumatic Stress Syndrome* (pp. 135–144). New York, NY: Plenum Publishing.

Hass, A. (1995). *The Aftermath: Living with the Holocaust.* New York, NY: Cambridge University Press.

Helmreich, W. (1992). *Against All Odds: Holocaust Survivors and the Successful Lives They Made in America.* New York, NY: Simon & Schuster.

Holmes, T.H. & Rahe, R.H. (1967). The social readjustment rating scale, *Journal of Psychosomatic Research,* 11 (2), 213–218.

Kahana, E., Fairchild, T., & Kahana, B. (1982). Adaptation. In D. Mangen & W. Peterson (Eds.), *Research Instruments in Social Gerontology: Clinical and Social Psychology, Vol 1* (pp. 145–193). Minneapolis, MN, University of Minnesota Press.

Kahana, B. & Kahana, E. (1998). Toward a temporal-spatial model of cumulative life stress: Placing late life stress effects in life course perspective. In J. Lomranz, (Ed.), *Handbook of Aging and Mental Health: An Integrative Approach* (pp. 153–178). New York, NY: Plenum Publishing Co.

Kahana, B. (2001). Isolation. In G. Maddox (Ed.) *The Encyclopedia of Aging*, (pp. 565–567). New York: Springer Publishing Company, Inc.

Kahana, B., Harel, Z., & Kahana, E. (1988). Predictors of Psychological Well-Being Among survivors of the Holocaust. In J. Wilson, Z. Harel, & B. Kahana (Eds.), *Human Adaptation to Extreme Stress: From the Holocaust to Vietnam* (pp. 171–192). New York: Plenum Publishing Co.

Kahana, E., Kahana, B., Harel, Z., & Rosner, T. (1988). Coping with Extreme Trauma. In J. Wilson, Z. Harel, & B. Kahana (Eds.), *Human Adaptation to Extreme Stress: From the Holocaust to Vietnam*, (pp. 55–79). New York, NY: Plenum Publishing Co.

Kahana, B. (1992). Late life Adaptation in the Aftermath of Extreme Stress. In M. Wykle, E. Kahana, & J. Kowal (Eds.), *Stress and Health Among the Elderly*. New York, NY: Springer.

Kahana, E., Redmond, C., Hill, G., Kahana, B., & Kercher, K. (1995). The effects of stress, vulnerability, and appraisals on the psychological well-being of the elderly, *Research on Aging*, 17 (4), 459–489.

Kahana, E., & Kahana, B. (2003). Contextualizing Successful Aging: New Directions in Age-Old Search. In R. Settersten, Jr. (Ed.). *Invitation to the Life Course: A New Look at Old Age*. (pp.225–255). Amityville, NY: Baywood Publishing Company.

Kahana, B., Kahana, E., Harel, Z., Kelly, K. Monaghan, P., & Holland, L. (1997). A framework for understanding the chronic stress of Holocaust survivors. In M. Gottlieb (Ed.), *Coping With Chronic Stress* (pp. 315–342). New York, NY: Plenum Publishing Co.

Kasl, S.V. (1992). Stress and Health Among the Elderly: Overview of Issues. In M. Wykle, E. Kahana, & J. Kowal (Eds.). *Stress and Health Among the Elderly*. New York: Springer.

Krause, N. (1991). Stressful events and life satisfaction among elderly men and women, *Journals of Gerontology*, 46 (2), S84–S92.

Krystal, H. (1968). Studies of Concentration Camp Survivors. In H. Krystal (Ed.), *Massive Psychic Trauma*, (pp. 23–46). New York: International Universities Press.

Lawton, M.P. (1975). The Philadelphia Geriatric Center Morale Scale: A Revision, *Journal of Gerontology*, 30(1), 85–89.

Lazarus, R.S. & Folkman, S. (1984). *Stress, Appraisal and Coping*. New York: Springer.

Lin, N. & Ensel, W.M. (1989). Life stress and health: Stressors and resources. *American Sociological Review*, 54 (3), 382–389.

Lomranz, R.J. (1990). Long-term Adaptation to Traumatic Stress in Light of Adult Development and Aging Perspectives. In M.A.P. Stephens, J.H. Crowther, S.E. Hobfoll, & D.L. Tennenbaum (Eds.), *Stress and Coping in Later Life Families* (pp. 99–121). New York: Hemisphere.

McCann, I. & Pearlman, L. (1990). *Psychological Trauma and the Adult Survivor: Theory, Therapy, and Transformation*. New York: Brunner/Mazel.

Nolen-Hoeksema, S., Morrow, J., Fredrickson, B. L. (1993). Response style and the duration of episodes of depressed mood. *Journal of Abnormal Psychology*, 102: 20–28.

Okun, M.A., Melichar, J.F., & Hill, M.D. (1990). Negative daily events, positive and negative social ties, and psychological distress among older adults, *Gerontologist*, 30 (2), 193–199.

Paivio, A. (1986). *Mental Representation: A Dual Coding Approach*. New York: Oxford University Press.

Pearlin, L.I. (1989). The sociological study of stress, *Journal of Health & Social Behavior*, 30 (3), 241–256.

Pearlin, L.I. & Mullan, J.T. (1992). Loss and Stress in Aging. In M. Wykle, E. Kahana, & J. Kowal (Eds.). *Stress and Health Among the Elderly*, (117–123). New York: Springer.

Portes, A. & Rumbaut, R. (1996). *Immigrant America: A Portrait*. Berkley, CA: University of California Press.

Raphael, B. (1986). *When Disaster Strikes: How Individuals and Communities Cope with Catastrophe*. New York: Basic Books.

Rosenbloom, M. (1985). The Holocaust survivor late in life. In G. Getzel & M. Mellor (Eds.), *Gerontological Social Work Practice in the Community.* (pp. 181–191). New York: Haworth Press.

Solomon, Z. (1995). From denial to recognition: Attitudes towards Holocaust survivors from WW II to the present , *Journal of Traumatic Stress,* 8(2), 215–228.

Solomon, Z. & Prager, E. (1992). Elderly Israeli Holocaust survivors during the Persian Gulf War: A study of psychological distress, *American Journal of Psychiatry,* 149 (12), 1707–1710.

Tanay, E. (2004). *Passport to Life: Autobiographical Reflections on the Holocaust.* Youngsville, NC: Forensic Press.

Wheaton, B. (1994). Sampling the Stress Universe. In W.R. Avison & I.H. Gotlib (Eds.). *Stress and Mental Health: Contemporary Issues and Prospects for the Future* (77–114). New York: Plenum Press.

Wheaton, B. (1997). The Nature of Chronic Stress. In B.H. Gottlieb (Ed.). *Coping with Chronic Stress,* (pp.43–74). New York: Plenum Press.

5

Physical Health of Holocaust Survivors and Immigrants in the U.S. and Israel

This chapter reviews conceptual perspectives and empirical findings on physical health of Holocaust survivors and immigrants in the United States and Israel. Initially, we review findings of prior studies on physical health sequelae of the Holocaust. Our second focus is on defining elements of physical health vulnerability and the measures we employed in this research to ascertain health status. Third, the focus shifts to examination of the empirical evidence on the health status of survivors and immigrants in the United States and Israel. Finally, the implications of the findings for the health vulnerability of elderly Holocaust survivors and their health care needs are discussed.

PRIOR RESEARCH ON PHYSICAL HEALTH OF HOLOCAUST SURVIVORS

Since survivors had experienced severe physical deprivation, starvation, and abuse by Nazi perpetrators, we were interested in determining the nature and extent of their chronic illness and physical symptoms at the time of our study which was conducted over forty years after the Holocaust. Early writings by Eitinger (1970) and others describe physical ailments endured by survivors immediately after World War II.

A number of follow-up medical studies were conducted on soldiers who had endured wartime stress (Wilson, Harel, Kahana, 1988). These studies have all demonstrated long term negative effects of wartime stress on the physical health of survivors including increased mortality. For example, Vietnam War veterans who exhibited symptoms of PTSD were twice as likely to have infectious diseases and nervous diseases and one and half times as likely to suffer from other diverse diseases (Bascarino, 1997). Since these studies have typically used different indices of physical health, data obtained are not always comparable.

The literature indicates that the adverse effects of a trauma experienced in an earlier part of the life span continue to adulthood and into old age. The synergistic effects of trauma exacerbate the normative mental and physical declines in old age (Landau & Litwin, 2000). For example, Golier, Yehuda, Lupien, Harvey, Grossman, & Elkin (2002) state that aging is associated with shrinkage (atrophy) in hippocampus and stress accelerates this process which results in faster decline in memory function of Holocaust survivors.

A review of the literature indicates that survivors of the Holocaust are especially vulnerable considering that they underwent physical assaults, diseases, malnutrition and psychological trauma. There has been relatively limited research done regarding the physical effects of extreme stress as compared to mental health effects of extreme trauma experienced by Holocaust survivors. Nevertheless, existing studies indicate that survivors are more likely to have health related difficulties. They have poorer self-rated health, are more preoccupied with their physical health and use medical resources more often (Landau & Litwin, 2000; Trappler, Braunstein, Moskowitz, & Friedman, 2002; Yaari, Eisenberg & Adler, 1999). Amir and Lev-Wiesel (2001) also found that survivors with a "lost identity", i.e., survivors who do not know their original names, and family histories display significantly poorer physical health and physical quality of life. They exhibit increased somatization and reported more chronic pain, than do survivors who know their original identities.

Moreover, women survivors seem to be more at a disadvantage compared to male survivors. The differential stressors endured by women in diverse settings ranging from Ghettos and death camps to underground movements have now been documented (Tec, 2003). Consistent with gerontological research on gender differences in marital status the majority of elderly female Holocaust survivors are widowed. They have to cope with both the effects of trauma and the loss of their spouse and its psychological, social, economic consequences. Therefore, the long lasting effects of extreme trauma experienced earlier in life combine with age related normative stressors to create health difficulties (Landau & Litwin, 2000).

One of the interesting findings of Yaari, Eisenberg and Adler (1999) is that even though Holocaust survivors report higher levels of physical pain and a larger number of pain sites, they do not perceive themselves as physically disabled. On the contrary, they report higher levels of function along various dimensions, such as distances walked or number of hours rest per day. This paradoxical finding may be a result of survivors' attempts to keep their minds off of their traumatic memories by maintaining an active life style. In addition, their early life experiences may have conditioned them to think that to be active is to be alive.

Shmotkin and Barilan (2002) also raise an important distinction regarding the physical health effects on elderly Holocaust survivors. They conceptualize the "place of Holocaust memories" in survivors' life as either present or past. They observe that if the survivor is "enmeshed" with past memories, is preoccupied with them and feels frustrated by all the losses experienced, s/he is likely to have poorer self-rated health, more somatization and more comorbidity. In contrast, if the survivor is able to contain the traumatic memories and free himself or herself from the painful memories of the past, s/he reports fewer diagnosed illnesses.

Literature also discusses the possible reactivation of trauma in the presence of a life threatening medical condition like cancer. Shmotkin and Barilan (2002) indicate that cancer patients who experienced the Holocaust show higher distress, poorer adaptation and coping strategies as compared to cancer patients who have not experienced a previous trauma in their life.

Prior research thus confirms the expectation of long term adverse physical health effects of the traumatic past of Holocaust survivors. Such sequelae are due to assaults on the body at the time of the Holocaust such as malnutrition or living in unsanitary conditions. These earlier traumas may continue affect the health of the survivors in their old age, at a time when all individuals encounter normative age related health challenges.

DEFINING HEALTH VULNERABILITY

Vulnerability entails being at risk for various health related declines and deterioration. In later life, health becomes significantly more vulnerable because of age associated increases in chronic illnesses, impairment and disability (Verbrugge and Jette, 1994). Physical health problems are more likely to occur, along with declining functional competence, necessitating greater dependence on informal caregivers and/or service providers. In addition, health vulnerability may lead to changes in living arrangements, including, the need for moves to sheltered care and nursing home placement. Lastly, greater health vulnerability includes greater risk of mortality (Townsend and Harel, 1990).

The health of older persons has traditionally been viewed from two perspectives: the medical perspective, emphasizing the presence or absence of disease; and the functional perspective, focusing on the ability of an aged individual to function effectively (Maddox, Clark, & Steinhauser, 1994). This chapter discusses health vulnerability, not only in terms of the prevalence of disease, impairment, disability, and functional limitations, but also considering factors that influence the health status of the aged. Although health risks increase with age, they are neither inevitable nor universal. Thus, health vulnerability is a multidimensional and dynamic concept. Such a framework acknowledges that some older people's health is more vulnerable than that of others, some aspects of health may be more susceptible to impairment than others, and may fluctuate over time. Health status at any given time is a reflection of complex age-related and/or time-dependent processes (Manton & Soldo, 1985) that may indicate either normal changes or pathology (Brody, 1985). Furthermore, the need for health services and for long-term care services is determined in part by objective health vulnerability and in part by subjective perceptions of health by the aged and those who care for them (Borawski, Kinney, & Kahana, 1996).

The incidence of physical health conditions and illness increases with age. Within this aggregate-trend, however, there are considerable individual variations, with many among the oldest-old in good health (Hogan, MacKnight, & Bergman, 2003). In addition to not being universal, many of the physical health problems associated with age are reversible. The physical ailments of older people are predominantly chronic rather than acute, and multiple conditions are the norm (Longino & Soldo, 1987).

In addition to specific measures of physical health conditions and impairments, global assessments of older persons' health are another way of measuring health vulnerability. Although these assessments are generally obtained through older persons' self-evaluations of their overall health on a rating scale, other observers (e.g., a nurse, physician, or family member) sometimes provide such assessments. Other common variations include comparative health assessments, where health at present is compared with how it was in the past or with the health of others. Most older people rate their health as good, very good, or excellent. Researchers have been intrigued by the importance of subjective health appraisals in predicting mortality (Idler & Benyamini, 1997). People over 65, at times, rate their health more positively than do younger people, despite also reporting more sick days, chronic health conditions, and sensory/motor impairments. Various explanations for this discrepancy have been offered. One reason may be that older people are less likely than younger people to interpret symptoms such as weakness and aches as signs of illness (Townsend & Harel, 1990).

Many older people believe that symptoms they perceive as minor or chronic are simply normal or at least inevitable signs of aging rather than illness or impairment. Another reason that older people may assess their health more positively is their perception that they are better off than other aged (Brody, 1985). At the same time, older adults worry more about their health than do middle-aged or younger adults and think of their health as more vulnerable (Townsend & Harel, 1990).

APPROACHES OF OUR STUDY

In the current study, we were able to utilize a broad-spectrum of physical health measures, which elicited responses regarding varied symptoms and disorders as well as the self-assessment of health. An additional strength of this study is the ability to compare the presence/absence and severity of disorders with our comparison group. Lastly, a comparison of health status of Holocaust survivors and immigrants in Israel as well as in the U.S. provides us with a rich cross-cultural comparison. It enables us to understand health status within different cultural contexts.

Since much of the early work done on Holocaust survivors has documented health problems among this group (Eitinger, 1970), we wanted to learn more about the prevalence of health conditions and symptomatology by utilizing standardized health measures and inventories employed in gerontological research.

The OARS Physical Health Inventory (Blazer, 1978) was used in this study along with several additional general physical health measures. The OARS Inventory has been used in a number of studies of older persons, including the Duke University Survey of the Elderly and the Cleveland General Accounting Office Study (Fillenbaum, 1984). The OARS version we used consists of a list of 26 health symptoms and diagnostic entities such as the presence or absence of arthritis, emphysema, cancer, liver disease etc. In addition, we have elaborated on these items and asked respondents who endorsed having a condition, to what extent that condition interferes with their functioning (from none to a great deal). Respondents were also asked to provide subjective assessments of their overall health using a two-item self-rated health index. Sensory impairments including adequacy of hearing and vision were also elicited. Health care utilization was also assessed in terms of both ambulatory physician visits and hospitalizations. Further indicators of health status included number of sick days at home during the past year, and number of different prescriptions and over the counter medications used.

Comparing Health of Survivors with Health of Immigrants

Summary of Health Behavior Measures

Table 1 summarizes our research findings relevant to self rated indicators of health, specific days of illness, physician visits, hospitalization episodes and use of medications. On global health measures that included self rated health and health compared with that of others there were significant differences found between survivors and immigrants, both in the U.S. and Israel. When respondents compared their own health with that of others of similar age, survivors rated themselves as having significantly poorer health than did immigrants in both the United States and Israel. On self-rated health immigrants rated themselves somewhat better than survivors in the United States (p < .05), while in Israel, somewhat unexpectedly, survivors rated themselves as having fewer health problems (p < .01). There was also a significant difference found between survivors and immigrants in their perceived illness severity (p < .01) with survivors indicating greater severity both in the U.S. and Israel. There were no significant differences found between survivors and immigrants in the number of visits to a physician, or in the number of hospitalizations over the last six months. However, survivors in the U.S. reported significantly (p < .01) more sick days during the past six months than did immigrants.

Table 1. Comparison of Self Rated Health Indicators and Health Related Behaviors Among Survivors and Immigrants Living in the U.S. and Israel

		Survivors		Immigrants	
		Mean	SD	Mean	SD
Self-rated health	U.S.	2.80	0.81	2.67	0.77*
problems	Israel	2.50	0.79	2.95	0.73**
Health compared	U.S	3.16	0.89	3.53	0.73**
that of others	Israel	3.31	0.80	3.72	0.77**
Illness Severity	U.S	5.90	4.80	4.90	3.80**
	Israel	4.40	4.80	3.40	3.40**
Sick days	U.S	6.91	17.70	3.19	10.20**
	Israel	5.65	13.12	5.88	13.60
Physician Visit	U.S	3.04	6.06	3.05	5.04
	Israel	4.87	6.08	4.43	7.15
Hospitalized	U.S	1.07	3.80	1.39	6.40
	Israel	1.74	7.60	1.71	5.38
Medications	U.S	1.39	1.46	1.86	1.94
	Israel	1.76	1.66	1.53	1.59

SPECIFIC HEALTH CONDITIONS

Specific health problems ascertained in this research included sensory problems, cardiovascular conditions, gastrointestinal problems, respiratory problems and other skeletal and bodily conditions as summarized in Table 2. Overall, survivors were found to have higher incidence of health conditions compared with the immigrants both in the United States and Israel; however the differences were generally small.

Skeletal Problems, Circulation and Arthritic Conditions: Among the U.S. respondents, we found significant differences between survivors and immigrants with the latter faring better on skeletal problems (p < .01), arthritic conditions (p < .05) and circulatory problems (p < .01). In Israel, no differences were found between the two groups on reported incidence of skeletal problems and circulation.

Sensory Impairments: Few differences were found in the United States between survivors and immigrants on sensory impairments, eyesight, glaucoma and hearing. In Israel, sensory problems and vision impairments were reported more frequently by survivors compared to immigrants (p < .01). However, no differences were reported in hearing problems or in incidence of glaucoma.

Cardiovascular Health Problems: On cardiovascular health problems such as blood pressure, heart trouble, stroke, and anemia, there were no significant differences found between survivors and immigrants in the United States. In Israel, survivors were found to have significantly (p < .01) more cardiovascular problems, however, on blood pressure, heart trouble, anemia and stroke no differences were found between the two groups.

Gastrointestinal Problems: On digestive disorders survivors in both the U.S. (p < .05) and Israel (p < .01) indicated having more problems compared to immigrants. More survivors, compared with immigrants in the U.S., indicated having diabetes (p < .01) and ulcers (p < .01). However, no differences were found between the two groups on incidence of liver and kidney disease. In Israel, conversely, no significant differences were found between the two groups in reported incidence of diabetes and ulcers, while liver disease and kidney disease survivors reported higher incidence (p < .05).

Other Health Conditions: Differences between survivors and immigrants were also ascertained on additional/illness categories. On allergies, US survivors reported more incidence than immigrants (p < .01). However, no differences were reported by respondents in Israel. On asthma, emphysema, and tuberculosis, both U.S. and Israeli survivors and immigrants reported similarly low incidence. On aggregate, no significant differences were found on urological problems and prostate problems between survivors

Table 2. Comparison of Specific Health Problems for Survivors and Immigrants Living in the U.S. and Israel

		Survivors		Immigrants	
		Mean	SD	Mean	SD
Skeletal Problems	U.S.	4.13	3.62	2.84	3.03**
	Israel	2.68	2.74	2.28	2.54
Circulatory problems	U.S	0.41	0.49	0.20	0.40**
	Israel	0.28	0.45	0.20	0.40
Arthritis/Rheumatism	U.S	2.40	1.22	1.95	1.05*
	Israel	1.63	1.09	1.41	0.91*
Sensory Problems	U.S	1.45	2.27	1.30	1.83
	Israel	3.17	2.61	2.25	1.62*
Eyesight Problems	U.S	3.48	0.92	3.64	0.93
	Israel	3.72	0.78	4.00	0.83*
Glaucoma	U.S	0.03	0.17	0.06	0.23
	Israel	0.05	0.23	0.03	0.18
Hearing Problems	U.S	3.71	0.92	3.86	0.98
	Israel	3.82	1.88	4.00	0.90
Cardiovascular Problems	U.S	3.26	3.96	2.76	3.11
	Israel	3.98	3.37	2.92	2.74**
High Blood Pressure	U.S	0.31	0.46	0.33	0.47
	Israel	0.34	0.47	0.40	0.39
Heart Trouble	U.S	0.26	0.44	0.23	0.42
	Israel	0.29	0.45	0.28	0.45
Effects of Stroke	U.S.	0.02	0.15	0.01	0.08
	Israel	0.04	0.21	0.06	0.24
Anemia	U.S.	0.17	0.72	0.15	0.54
	Israel	0.10	0.43	0.06	0.31
Digestive problems	U.S	2.94	3.95	2.40	3.44*
	Israel	3.47	3.67	2.14	2.24**
Diabetes	U.S.	0.16	0.37	0.06	0.25**
	Israel	0.14	0.35	0.10	0.30
Ulcers	U.S.	0.18	0.38	0.05	0.22**
	Israel	0.15	0.35	0.09	0.29
Liver Disease	U.S.	0.02	0.13	0.02	0.14
	Israel	0.07	0.26	0.01	0.08**
Kidney Disease	U.S.	0.05	0.27	0.03	0.20
	Israel	0.11	0.31	0.03	0.16**
Allergies	U.S	3.38	1.84	2.94	1.47*
	Israel	0.74	1.44	0.63	1.17
Asthma	U.S	0.04	0.19	0.03	0.16
	Israel	0.07	0.26	0.06	0.25
Emphysema/Bronchitis	U.S	0.04	0.20	0.05	0.21
	Israel	0.00	0.15	0.01	0.11
Tuberculosis	U.S	0.00	0.00	0.02	0.14
	Israel	0.04	0.21	0.03	0.16
Urological problems	U.S	0.73	1.61	0.54	1.56
	Israel	0.45	0.96	0.42	1.01

Table 2. (*Cont.*)

		Survivors		Immigrants	
		Mean	SD	Mean	SD
Urinary Tract, Prostate	U.S.	0.15	0.35	0.15	0.35
	Israel	0.13	0.33	0.15	0.36
Cancer or Leukemia	U.S.	0.01	0.11	0.03	0.16
	Israel	0.01	0.10	0.04	0.21
Parkinson's Disease	U.S.	0.00	0.00	0.01	0.11
	Israel	0.02	0.13	0.01	0.11
Alzheimer's Disease	U.S.	0.00	0.00	0.01	0.08
	Israel	0.02	0.15	0.01	0.08

$*p < .05; **p < .01$

and immigrants in either the U.S. or Israel. No differences were found between survivors and immigrants in the U.S. and Israel on cancer, Parkinson's disease, or Alzheimer's disease.

DISCUSSION

There is clear indication in these data that older Holocaust survivors perceive their health generally and their health compared with the health status of their age peers to be worse than that of the immigrants in both countries. At the same time, these data indicate that the magnitude of the differences is generally small among our respondents. Furthermore, differences in the health problems are more discernable in self reported illness severity and are found in only few of the chronic health conditions. It is important to note that survivor participants in this research may represent persons who were originally in better health, as only a small fraction of European Jews survived the atrocities of the Holocaust. In addition, this research does not include the homebound, the institutionalized and those otherwise unable to participate in our research.

It is recognized that one cannot readily compare the early findings of Eitinger and others, based on the characteristics of survivors measured soon after the Holocaust with our findings forty-five years later. Furthermore, the medical questions asked within the framework of a social science interview represent a different type of assessment than a physical examination. Nevertheless, research has demonstrated that self-report indices of physical health correlate well with the findings of physician administered examinations (Ford, Follmar, Salmon, Medalie, & Roy, 1988).

The above differences in health are notable, however, in view of the fact that the immigrants in America are six years older than the American survivors and immigrants in Israel are four years older than the survivors. Despite the fact that survivors are younger by six years than the immigrants, overall survivors portray more physical health problems. Consequently, observations of higher incidences of specific chronic illnesses among survivors reflect conservative estimates when adjusted for age.

We note that in a number of specific areas, survivors in Israel seem to have fewer ailments than those in the U.S. This observation would suggest that living in Israel may serve as somewhat of a buffer against physical diseases. In some cases, it buffers both survivor and immigrant populations. In other cases, one notes interaction effects between immigrants and survivors, based on country of residence. Accordingly, our study findings are consistent with earlier research findings regarding areas of physical health vulnerability among survivors. At the same time, they also underscore the notion of selective vulnerability.

In interpreting our findings regarding physical health, it is important to recognize the diversity that characterizes the aged survivor and immigrant populations in both United States and Israel. Furthermore, it is notable, particularly in the area of physical health that these survivors who still function and live independently in the community reflect the hardiest and longest living among the victims of this trauma.

REFERENCES

Amir, M., & Lev-Wiesel, R. (2001). Does Everyone Have a Name? Psychological Distress and Quality of Life Among Child Holocaust Survivors with Lost Identity, *Journal of Traumatic Stress*, 14 (4), 859–869.

Bascarino, J.A. (1997). Diseases among men 20 years after exposure to severe stress: Implications for clinical research and medical care, *Psychosomatic Medicine*, 59, 605–614.

Blazer, D. (1978). The Durham Survey: Description and application. In *Multidimensional Functional Assessment-the OARS Methodology: A Manual.* (2nd Ed.). Durham, NC: Duke University Center for the Study of Aging and Human Development.

Borawski, E., Kinney, J., & Kahana, E. (1996). The Meaning of Older Adults' Health Appraisals: Congruence with Health Status and Determinant of Mortality. *Journal of Gerontology*, 51B(3), S157–S170.

Brody, E. (1985). *Mental and Physical Health Practices of Older Persons: A Guide for Health Professionals.* New York: Springer.

Eitinger, L. (1970). The concentration camp syndrome and its late sequelae. In J.E. Dimsdale (Ed.), *Survivors, Victims and Perpetrators: Essays on the Nazi Holocaust.* (pp 127–162). New York: Hemisphere.

Fillenbaum, G. (1984). *Assessing the Well-being of the Elderly: Why and How Functional Assessment is Being Done in the United States and Abroad.* Duke University Center for the Study of Aging.

Ford, A., Follmar, S., Salmon, R., Medalie, J., Roy, A., & Galaska, S. (1988). Health and function in the old and very old, *Journal of the American Geriatrics Society*, 36, 187–197.

Golier, J., Yehuda, R., Harvey, P., Grossman, R., & Elkin, A. (2002). Memory Performance in Holocaust Survivors with Posttraumatic Stress Disorder, *The American Journal of Psychiatry*, 159, 1682–1688.

Hogan, D.B. MacKnight, C. & Bergman, H. (2003). Model, Definitions, and Criteria of Frailty. *Aging Clinical and Experimental Research*, 15 (3), Suppl, 1–29.

Idler, E.L. & Benyamini, Y. (1997). Self-rated Health and Mortality: A Review of Twenty-seven Community Studies. *Journal of Health and Social Behavior*, 38 (1): 21–37.

Kane, R.A. & Kane, R.L. (1987). *Long-Term Care: Principles, Programs and Policies.* New York: Springer.

Landau, R., & Litwin, H. (2000). The Effects of Extreme Early Stress in Very Old Age, *Journal of Traumatic Stress*, 13 (3): 473–487.

Longino, C. & Soldo, B. (1987). The Graying of America: Implications of Life Extension on the Quality of Life. In R. Ward & S. Tobin (Eds.) *Health in Aging: Sociological Issues and Policy Directions.* (pp 58–85). New York: Springer.

Maddox, G. L., Clark, D.O., & Steinhauser, K. (1994). Dynamics of Functional Impairment in Late Adulthood. *Social Science and Medicine*, 38 (7), 925–936.

Manton, K. & Soldo, B. (1985). Dynamics of health changes in the oldest old: New perspectives and evidence, *The Milbank Memorial Fund Quarterly Health and Society*, 63 (2), 206–285.

Shanas, E., & Maddox, G. (1985). Health, Health Resources, and Utilization of Care. In R. Binstock & E. Shanas (Eds.). *Handbook of Aging and the Social Sciences.* New York: Van Nortstrand Reinhold.

Shmotkin, D., & Barilan, Y. M. (2002). Expressions of Holocaust Experience and Their Relationship to Mental Symptoms and Physical Morbidity among Holocaust Survivor Patients, *Journal of Behavioral Medicine*, 25 (2), 115–134.

Tec, N. (2003). *Resilience and Courage. Women, Men, and the Holocaust.* New Haven, CT: Yale University Press.

Townsend, A., & Harel, Z. (1990). Health vulnerability and service need among the aged. In Z. Harel, P. Ehrlich, & R. Hubbard (Eds.). *The Vulnerable Aged.* New York: Springer.

Trappler, B., Braunstein, J., Moskowitz, G., & Friedman, S. (2002). Holocaust Survivors in a Primary Care Setting: Fifty Years Later, *Psychological Reports*, 91: 545–552.

Verbrugge, L.M. & Jette, A.M. (1994). The Disablement Process. *Social Science Medicine*, 38 (1), 1–14.

Wilson, J., Harel, Z. & Kahana, B. (1988). *Human Adaptation and Coping: From Holocaust to Vietnam.* New York: Plenum.

Yaari, A., Eisenberg, E., Adler, R. (1999). Chronic Pain in Holocaust Survivors, *Journal of Pain and Symptom Management*, 17 (3), 181–187.

6

Mental Health of Older Holocaust Survivors

The primary focus of this chapter is the mental health of Holocaust survivors and immigrants in the United States and Israel. First, the evolution of concern for the mental health of Holocaust survivors will be reviewed, followed by the review and discussion of the empirical findings from our cross-national research project. In our investigation of mental health of Holocaust survivors, we attempted to determine the prevalence, nature, and severity of psychiatric symptoms and psychological characteristics, which may distinguish survivors from a closely matched comparison group of immigrants of similar socio-cultural background.

Perhaps the most commonly accepted generalization regarding consequences of the trauma of the Holocaust relates to the expectation of enduring mental health consequences (Dohrenwend, 2000, Herman, 1992; Krell & Sherman, 1997). Such sequelae have long been reported by clinicians (Danieli, 1994; Krystal, 1968). Symptoms have been shown to persist, even many years past the original traumatization (Dasberg, 1987; Yehuda, Elkin, Binder-Brynes, Kahana, Southwick, Schneider and Giller, 1996). In this chapter we analyze mental health consequences observed in our research as we compare immigrants with survivors in detail.

We examine these consequences even while we recognize that our study considers these long term survivors who have managed to function successfully in the community. Therefore, we can only observe those psychological symptoms that are residual to the healing that might have taken place in the interim years. During this period, long-term survivors utilized, to the best of their abilities, protective resources of coping strategies, personality strengths, as well as social supports.

Based on survivor accounts and psychiatric evaluations of those survivors seeking help or compensation after the Holocaust, an extensive psychodynamic literature documented severe psychiatric damage, referred to as Concentration Camp or "KZ" Syndrome (Chodoff, 1963; Krystal, 1968; Niederland, 1981). Case studies revealed chronic states of depression and anxiety, inability to enjoy life, survivor guilt, and unresolved grief. Hyperamnesia, or inability to suppress memories of persecution, was also reported. These clinical studies were subsequently critiqued on the basis of bias resulting from: 1. their focus on clinical populations, 2. their lack of reliance on standard and replicable assessment techniques, 3. the absence of control groups, and 4. their failure to focus on coping and strengths of larger cross-sections of survivors (Harel, Kahana, & Kahana, 1988).

Holocaust survivors who were treated in Oslo psychiatric facilities shortly after the war were found to exhibit significant somatic and psychological scars (Eitinger, 1980; Eitinger & Strom, 1973). Community surveys of non-clinical populations of Holocaust survivors were initiated in the United States, Canada, and Israel mostly during the 1980s, almost 40 years after the trauma. In an early study-based on survivors and a comparison group of immigrants to Canada, Eaton, Sigal, and Weinfeld (1982) observed significant elevations in psychological symptoms among survivors, using the Langner index of mental health. Four or more symptoms were reported by 43% of survivors, compared with 28% in the comparison group.

A larger community-based study of Holocaust survivors in Israel was reported by Carmil and Carel (1986). On the basis of selected questions from the Cornell Medical Index, small but statistically significant differences in psychological distress were found between survivors and the comparison group. Thirty-three percent of survivors reported three or more areas of distress, compared with 25% among respondents in the comparison group. Specific psychological problems, such as sleep disturbances (Lavie, 2001) and dissociations (Yehuda et al., 1996) have been documented among Holocaust survivors.

Few reports in the literature on the mental health of Holocaust survivors use formal criteria for posttraumatic stress disorder (PTSD). In Kuch and Cox's (1992) study of 124 Holocaust survivors, 46.8% met the criteria for PTSD according to the third edition of the *Diagnostic and Statistical Manual of Mental Disorders* (DSM-III; American Psychiatric Association, 1980). In a small-scale study of Holocaust survivors in Poland, PTSD symptoms, based on DSM-III-Revised (American Psychiatric Association, 1987), were found in all the survivors who were assessed (Orwid, Domagalska, & Pietruzewski, 1995).

Taken together, diverse studies considering the psychological impact of the Holocaust among long-term survivors reveal a consistent picture of a small, but statistically significant, elevation in indicators of psychological distress. Nevertheless, there is a noteworthy overlap in distributions between survivors and normal non-traumatized comparison groups.

Our comparative study of Holocaust survivors and immigrants in two different cultures (United States and Israel) enabled us to study the impact of cultural and geographical factors on mental health. Thus, survivors of the Holocaust who live in Israel, a war torn country, were expected to have more mental health problems compared with those who live in the United States, where objective stressors have been far fewer. We expected exacerbation of mental health symptoms among Holocaust survivors in Israel. On the other hand, the culture in Israel provides social supports and a clear recognition of the Holocaust through its annual commemoration day (Yom Hashoah) and through many other symbols and ceremonies relevant to survivorship. These considerations would lead us to expect living in Israel to serve as a buffer of sorts that may ameliorate adverse mental health effects of Holocaust trauma.

RESEARCH FINDINGS

We will present our findings based on the following measures used in this study: the Lawton Morale Scale (Lawton, 1975); the Symptom Distress Scale (SCL-90); and a Holocaust-specific symptom scale, which we developed and called the Traumatization Measure. While our study did not use a specific PTSD scale, our interview questions and instruments elicited information to assess symptoms of traumatic stress reactions.

LAWTON MORALE SCALE

The Lawton Morale Scale, which was developed at the Philadelphia Geriatric Center (Lawton, 1975), was utilized with this sample to determine the level of morale, life satisfaction, and coping with aging, as survivors grow older. This scale typically yields three subconstructs in factor analytic studies: life satisfaction, agitation, and attitudes about aging (Harel & Deimling, 1984; Mangen & Peterson, 1982).

Survivors were found to have significantly lower mean (i.e., average) morale scores than immigrants in both the U.S. and Israel. U.S. survivors had an average morale score of 8.17 in contrast to 10.48 for U.S. immigrants. Israeli survivors were found to have an average of score of 9.31 in contrast to 10.99 for Israeli immigrants. Both of these differences were small, but statistically significant at the .001 level. A perusal of these mean scores reveals that U.S. survivors are the group suffering the most from low morale. Unexpectedly, both survivors and immigrants living in Israel showed higher morale than their U.S. counterparts. These data underscore that the mental health of the survivors was clearly adversely affected by their traumatic experiences. However, postwar life in Israel had some beneficial features, allowing for higher morale in spite of the stresses experienced by those residing in a less affluent and less peaceful environment. These features may include social support and feeling of belongingness.

Further insight into the nature of mental health symptoms, as reflected by the Morale Scale, come to light as we peruse the frequencies of endorsing individual items and patterns suggested within the three morale subscales shown in Table 1.

Table 1. Lawton Morale Scale

	Survivors	Immigrants	P
Life Satisfaction			
1. Feel lonely a lot	%	%	Sig.
U.S.	41.2	20.8	.001
Israel	34.3	25.3	.07
2. See enough of friends, relatives			
U.S.	70.9	64.1	.19
Israel	84.8	78.3	.24
3. Feel life isn't worth living anymore			
U.S.	26.2	14.2	.01
Israel	26.1	14.6	.01
4. Have a lot to be sad about			
U.S.	65.6	26.1	.001
Israel	54.1	44.8	.05
5. Life is hard much of time			
U.S.	49.1	13.6	.001
Israel	33.3	19.0	.003
6. Satisfied with life			
U.S	85.4	86.7	.76
LMS15	72.4	86.3	.002
Agitation			
1. Little things bother more this year			
U.S.	42.9	25.2	.001
Israel	40.0	30.8	.08
2. Sometimes worry, can't sleep			
U.S.	57.0	25.5	.001
Israel	51.9	26.3	.001
3. Afraid of a lot of things			
U.S.	34.0	11.0	.001
Israel	36.5	12.8	.001

Table 1. (*Cont.*)

	Survivors	Immigrants	P
4. Get mad more than I used to			
U.S.	27.3	11.6	.001
Israel	35.7	28.2	.14
5. Take things hard			
U.S.	63.4	42.7	.001
Israel	42.4	32.5	.06
6. Get upset easily			
U.S.	60.5	33.3	.001
Israel	51.0	43.3	.22
Attitudes About Aging			
1. Things worse with age			
U.S.	51.9	42.0	.08
Israel	65.1	47.6	.002
2. Less pep than last year			
U.S.	46.0	35.5	.06
Israel	51.4	55.9	.40
3. As you get older, feel less useful			
U.S.	31.9	39.2	.17
Israel	47.0	46.8	.97
4. As you get older, things are better			
U.S.	50.0	43.8	.29
Israel	33.5	34.8	.82
5. Happy now as when young			
U.S.	51.3	42.5	.12
LMS10	43.5	46.9	.54

LIFE SATISFACTION SUBSCALE

We notice an interesting pattern on the Life Satisfaction subscale. It is evident that survivors are still mourning their losses, with 66% of U.S. survivors and 54% of Israeli survivors reporting that "they have a lot to be sad about". Furthermore, a notable minority of 26% of survivors in both the U.S. and Israel state that "life is not worth living", suggesting depressive symptoms. This is almost twice the number showing depressive ideation among immigrants in both countries. Survivors in both countries are more likely to feel lonely than immigrants. Furthermore, survivors in the U.S. are far more likely to feel lonely than the survivors or immigrants in Israel. These findings may suggest the protective features of life in Israel. Thus, social integration of both immigrants and survivors may be the mechanism underlying lesser symptomatology among Israeli survivors.

In spite of the above noted differences in levels of morale, the item about general life satisfaction is endorsed by a very high proportion of respondents, with 85% of survivors and 87% of immigrants in the U.S. stating that they are satisfied with life. Israeli immigrants are similar to those in the U.S. (86%), but fewer survivors in Israel endorse the overall life satisfaction item (72%). Perhaps, the life satisfaction item reflects the appreciation of life and even gratefulness of those who survived. Thus our data reveal the complexities of our survivor vulnerability and resilience. Survivors are still haunted by their fears and losses, and yet they are immensely appreciative of what life has to offer.

AGITATION SUBSCALE

In considering items on the "agitation" subscale, we see a consistent pattern of significantly greater manifestation of anxiety on all items for survivors in the U.S. as compared to U.S. immigrants. Thus, it is notable that, in the U.S., 63% of survivors report "taking things hard" compared to 43% of the immigrants. 34% of U.S. survivors report being "afraid of a lot of things", compared to only 11% of U.S. immigrants reporting such fears. Similar patterns are observed for the Israel based respondents, where fears are reported by almost three times as many survivors than by immigrants (36% versus 13%). With the exception of fears and the tendency to experience anger (get mad easily) survivors living in Israel show lower levels of agitation than their U.S. based counterparts. At the same time, immigrants living in Israel show more agitation than U.S. immigrants. Consequently, differences between survivors and immigrants on agitation are significant on only three of the six subscale items. The cultural climate of Israel generally elicits stronger emotional responses of its inhabitants. Yet, once again, it is likely that the sense of emotional security of living among one's own people helps buffer the experience of agitation among survivors.

ATTITUDES ABOUT AGING SUBSCALE

With regard to attitudes toward aging, we found little difference between survivors and immigrants in the U.S. or in Israel. It is noteworthy that 51% of U.S. based survivors report feeling as happy as when they were young compared to 43% of U.S. based immigrants. Asking survivors to look at changes in their lives, relative to the past, invites them to balance positive aspects of healing and growing distance from their traumatic past, against increasing frailty and losses that may be associated with aging. The generally positive outlook of survivors in evaluating their aging is also reflected in our findings that about half of the survivors both in the U.S. and in Israel considered themselves to have as much pep as they did last year. However, we must also note that immigrants in our sample were somewhat older than our survivors and that the greater relative youth of our survivors could be masking some potential differences in attitudes toward aging. All in all, aging represents as much a triumph as a threat for those people who had been destined for extermination.

SYMPTOM CHECK LIST SCL-90

This scale, based on work of Derogatis (1983), was employed to compare the mental health/psychopathology of Holocaust survivors with immigrant respondents in both the United States and Israel. In earlier years, clinicians working with Holocaust survivors who sought professional help determined the nature and degree of their psychopathology through non-quantitative analyses, based on their clinical observations (Kahana, Harel, & Kahana, 1988). This study aimed to quantify both degree and type of psychological symptomatology of Holocaust survivors and of the immigrant comparison groups. The SCL-90 has been frequently used with traumatized populations, including natural disaster survivors and Vietnam veterans (Lindy, Green, & Wilson, 1988). This enables us to eventually compare survivors on the same instrument with members of other groups.

It is interesting to note that the Lawton Morale Scale correlates rather highly with the total SCL-90 score as well as with subscores. It is, nevertheless, important to include the SCL-90 data on these groups since the latter measure gives us detailed scores on major diagnostic entities and distress categories of the scale (e.g. somatization, depression, etc.).

Findings indicate significantly ($p < .001$) greater "psychopathology" among survivors than immigrants, both in the U.S. and in Israel. However, the vast majority of survivors and immigrants in both countries portrayed relatively low scores on all the SCL-90 subscales. This is an important observation which has not been available in past research where investigators were eager to portray significant differences, but in so doing, overlooked the fact that most survivors do not depict extreme or even moderate psychopathology. The results from the findings on the subscales follow. It should be noted that we scored each SCL item on a 1–5 Likert scale as opposed to a 0–4 scale because of computational reasons. Therefore, the averages in our group

Table 2. Symptom Check List SCL-90

	Survivors		Immigrants		
	Mean	St. Dev.	Mean	St. Dev.	P
Somatization					
U.S	22.50	9.42	16.33	5.12	.001
Israel	21.55	9.42	16.33	5.12	.001
Obsessiveness					
U.S	18.90	7.39	14.45	4.16	.001
Israel	17.26	7.26	14.11	4.39	.001
Sensitivity					
U.S	13.89	4.57	11.45	2.90	.001
Israel	13.17	4.83	11.32	3.12	.01
Depression					
U.S	25.82	10.67	20.74	7.49	.001
Israel	21.71	8.94	17.21	4.85	.001
Anxiety					
U.S	18.69	8.61	13.15	4.17	.001
Israel	16.67	6.98	12.92	3.61	.001
Hostility					
U.S	8.97	3.25	7.19	1.95	.001
Israel	9.11	3.65	7.43	2.19	.001
Phobia					
U.S	9.92	4.34	7.82	1.77	.001
Israel	9.49	3.65	8.57	2.19	.01
Paranoia					
U.S	9.45	3.24	7.19	1.68	.001
Israel	8.64	3.70	7.78	2.65	.05
Pychoticism					
U.S	13.59	4.18	11.30	2.20	.001
Israel	12.27	3.86	11.13	1.80	.001

should be higher than the averages of other groups, which used the 0–4 Likert scale. Table 2 provides data comparing survivors and immigrants on SCL subscales. Ranges for each subscale were from 10–50.

Somatization: American survivors portrayed significantly (p < .001) higher indications of somatization than did U.S. immigrants. Israeli survivors also had significantly (p < .001) higher reported incidence on this subscale than Israeli immigrants. There was very little difference found by country between survivors or immigrants in the two countries.

Obsession: Findings from our research indicate that the U.S. survivors portrayed significantly (p < .001) higher obsessive responses than did immigrants. In Israel, survivors also had significantly (p < .001) higher obsessive responses than immigrants. There were no significant differences in responses in the two countries.

Interpersonal sensitivity: Our research findings indicate that U.S. survivors show significantly (p < .001) higher interpersonal sensitivity responses than immigrants. In Israel, survivors also had significantly (p = .01) higher sensitivity responses than immigrants. There were no significant differences of either survivors or immigrants in responses within the two countries.

Depression: A review of our findings indicated that survivors in the United States were significantly (p = .001) more depressed than immigrants. Similarly, survivors in Israel were found to have significantly (p < .001) higher depression than immigrants. Both survivors and immigrants in the United States portrayed higher depressive symptoms that did respondents in the respective groups in Israel.

Anxiety: In the U.S. survivors' responses indicate significantly (p < .001) more anxiety compared with the responses of immigrants. In Israel, survivors also portrayed somewhat more anxiety than did immigrants. There was little country difference found in the responses of immigrants on this subscale. However, among survivors, there appeared to be a somewhat higher degree of anxiety in the United States compared with survivors living in Israel.

Hostility: Survivors indicated slightly higher hostility scores than immigrants in both the United States and Israel. No differences were found in the responses of participants in our research in the two countries.

Phobic Reaction: In both the United States and Israel survivors' responses indicated significantly (p < .001 and p < .01) higher phobic reaction than did immigrants, with greater difference found between survivors and immigrants in the U.S. However, the magnitude of differences between these two groups is small.

Paranoid Ideations: In the U.S. survivors' responses indicate significantly (p < .001) more paranoid ideations, compared with the responses of immigrants. In Israel survivors also indicated more (p < .05) paranoid ideations than did immigrants. The magnitude of differences between these two groups is small. U.S. survivors portrayed slightly more paranoia than Israeli survivors, but Israeli immigrants show slightly more than their American counterparts.

Psychoticism Scale: Survivors in both countries score significantly higher on the Psychotocism Scale than did immigrant respondents (p < .001). American survivors portrayed more such symptoms than Israeli survivors.

In evaluating these differences it is important to note that levels of symptoms were very low on most subscales. The significantly higher incidence of symptomatology among survivors in the context of generally low scores may be due to a small number of highly affected individuals, who indeed may manifest mental health problems and whose impact is reflected in the mean scores of the entire group. It is also noteworthy that there were few differences based on country of residence between either survivors or immigrants.

TRAUMATIZATION ITEMS

Questions in this measure elicit responses concerning respondents' ability to enjoy life, to have a good time, to trust people, and to express anger. Other questions included nightmares or repetitive dreams. The above variables have been considered during the decades of the 1950s through the early 80s, by clinicians specializing in the treatment of Holocaust survivors, as characteristics of the KZ syndrome (concentration camp syndrome) (Krystal, 1988).

As indicated in Table 3, survivors show significantly more psychiatric symptoms on this measure compared with immigrant respondents ($p < .001$). There is a significant difference between survivors and immigrants on these variables including nightmares and repetitive dreams, inability to have a good time, and inability to trust people. With regard to the ability to enjoy themselves and to express anger, survivors also show greater symptomatology, and the findings approach significance. Even the more supportive milieu of Israel is unable to completely buffer against nightmares and repetitive dreams. Nevertheless, the percentage of survivors who report nightmares and dreams "often or very often" is lower among respondents

Table 3. Traumatization Items*

		Survivors		Immigrants		
		Mean	St. Dev.	Mean	St. Dev.	P
Unable to enjoy yourself	U.S	2.59	.097	2.08	0.91	.001
	Israel	2.59	1.22	2.07	1.17	.09
Unable to experience anger	U.S	1.89	1.07	1.69	0.85	.07
	Israel	2.13	1.24	1.89	1.15	.08
Unable to trust people	U.S	2.65	1.17	2.02	0.74	.001
	Israel	2.34	1.20	2.05	1.11	.02
Unable to have a good time	U.S	2.42	1.07	2.09	0.91	.01
	Israel	2.30	1.25	1.93	1.18	.01
Having nightmares and	U.S	2.93	1.23	1.64	0.99	.001
repetitive dreams	Israel	2.16	1.38	1.46	0.89	.001

* scores for each item range from 1 to 5

living in Israel than in the American sample. These findings, once again, are contrary to the cumulative stress hypothesis, which would lead us to expect Israel based survivors to exhibit more evidence of traumatization.

SUMMARY OF FINDINGS AND CONCLUSIONS

This study remains unique in its simultaneous focuses on psychological distress among Holocaust survivors as well as a comparison group, both in the U.S. and in Israel. In terms of psychological distress, survivors' SCL-90 symptom profiles were elevated relative to both comparison participants and standardized norms. In terms of morale, responses to Lawton's 17-item Morale Scale indicated differences between the survivor and comparison groups on seven of the 17 items. Although statistically significant differences were found between survivors and immigrants, in the direction of greater symptomatology, emotional distress, and lower morale among the survivors, the percentage differences are not large and there is considerable overlap between survivors and immigrants on several of the mental health scales. Indeed some survivors portray less symptomatology than some immigrants. Such overlap in distributions raises an important note of caution against stereotyping the "typical" survivor as being psychologically impaired.

A variety of explanations have been proposed to account for the psychological well-being and absence of adverse outcomes among a significant number of survivors of extreme trauma (Antonovsky, 1979; Landau & Litwin, 2000). One explanation relates to selective long-term survival of those with the greatest resiliency and personality resources prior to the trauma. A second observation relates to the inoculation effect of extreme stress, which may result in greater hardiness in facing stress subsequent to the trauma (Kobasa, Maddi & Kahn, 1982). It may also be argued that supportive personal and socio-cultural environments, which buffered the ill effects of trauma, aided survivors (Herman, 1992). Finally, positive long-term outcomes may also be attributed to the success of the healing process, which permits positive affective states to emerge subsequent to trauma (Gill, 1988). Clinical psychologists may attribute these to the regenerative powers of the ego (Rappaport, 1968); whereas sociologists or social psychologists point to the healing powers of social integration and support (Harel and Noelke, 1982; George, 1990), and/or finding meaning in adversity (Kahana et al., 1989; Marcus & Rosenberg, 1988).

The State of Israel serves as a buffer in softening the blow of the Holocaust on the mental health of survivors. Survivors living in Israel seem to fare better than American survivors on some of our test variables. This is particularly evident on the Traumatization measure. It appears that the existence of both macro support systems and micro support systems in Israel constitute buffering agents. Thus, special holidays and commemorations relative to Holocaust survivorship are celebrated every year. On a family and personal level, most Israeli families have one or more relatives who are Holocaust survivors. Furthermore, the strong Jewish identity found in Israel, coupled with the fact that the Israeli nation is surviving, growing, and developing despite sustained threats by surrounding countries, serves to bolster morale, self-confidence, pride, and overall well-being among Holocaust survivors. Our earlier hypotheses were that Israeli survivors of the Holocaust would portray greater emotional distress than American Holocaust survivors because Israeli survivors have to continuously face the threat of annihilation by its hostile neighbors. Thus, they can no longer live in peace even after the Holocaust. This ongoing stress should have had a cumulative negative effect on Israeli Holocaust survivors, in contrast to the more tranquil environment in which American survivors live. Our data however suggest that this cumulative stress is counteracted by the strong social and emotional support system, which surround Holocaust survivors in Israel.

In considering the relative psychological intactness of Holocaust survivors, it should be recognized that we must look beyond outcomes of trauma, such as PTSD, and focus on the healing journey required of survivors as they move on with their lives (Gill, 1988; Sadavoy, 1997). This temporal contextual emphasis has also allowed for a closer look at the stages of the post-Holocaust journey. Our data raise some very important questions about approaches of the mental health literature that categorizes people, based on meeting criteria of various diagnostic entities, such as Post Traumatic Stress Disorder or depression. According to these psychiatric approaches, one could either be mentally ill or have an absence of mental illness (Yehuda et al., 1996). A second approach, that is more prevalent in social science research, takes an incremental view of mental health symptomatology. Thus, people can have lower or higher scores on depressive symptoms or on anxiety scales without reaching the diagnostic criteria for a disorder. It is assumed that those with higher scores are worse off than those with lower scores, even in the absence of a diagnostic label (Dohrenwend, 2000).

A careful consideration of feeling states reported by Holocaust survivors points to the need for a more textured consideration of what are traditionally viewed as mental health symptoms. Responses regarding items reflecting fear, hurt and loss clearly support the view that extreme trauma results in the long-term experience of these emotions. However, consideration of the life experiences endured by these now elderly human beings, much earlier in their lives, leads us to view their continuing memories and emotions as reflecting the humanity and sensitivity of those who survived the atrocities. Their continuing grief and sense of loss must also be juxtaposed against their repeated expressions of optimism about the future and their overall life satisfaction, even in old age. Perhaps it is time that we rethink our evaluation of such mixed emotions among survivors and start viewing them as expressions of normalcy and even transcendence in the aftermath of trauma (Tornstam, 1992). Thus, many long term survivors who have successfully dealt with life challenges do not exhibit 'numbing' or 'avoidance' and can express their continuing grief, while at the same time they appreciate their individual as well as collective national survival (Sadavoy, 1997).

Tormstam's (1992) notion of 'gerotranscendence' may come closest to describing the mental health of these long term survivors. They are, in every sense of the word, 'survivors'. They are physically and socially well functioning but wounded story tellers as described by Frankl (1984). They must continue, as a matter of conscience, to bear witness about their wounds and keep telling their story. But, they are doing so to build a better tomorrow for themselves, for their families and for society at large.

REFERENCES

American Psychiatric Association (1980). *Diagnostic criteria from DSM-III.* Washington: American Psychiatric Association.

American Psychiatric Association (1987). *Diagnostic criteria from DSM-III-R.* Washington: American Psychiatric Association.

Antonovsky, A (1979). *Health, Stress, and Coping.* San Francisco: Jossey Bass.

Carmil, D., & Carel, R. (1986). Emotional distress and satisfaction in life among Holocaust survivors-A community study of survivors and controls, *Psychological Medicine*, 16, 141–149.

Chodoff, P. (1963). Late effects of the concentration camp syndrome. *Archives of General Psychiatry*, 8, 323–333.

Danieli, Y. (1994). Countertransference, Trauma, and Training. In J.P. Wilson & J.D. Lindy (Eds.). *Countertransference in the Treatment of PTSD.* New York: Guilford Press.

Dasberg, H. (1987). Psychological distress of Holocaust survivors and offspring in Israel, forty years later: A review. *Israel Journal of Psychiatry & Related Sciences*, 24(4), 243–256.

Dohrenwend, B. (2000). The role of adversity and stress in psychopathology: Some evidence and its implications for theory and research, *Journal of Health and Social Behavior*, 41(1), 1–19.

Eaton, W., Sigal, J., & Weinfeld, M. (1982). Impairment of Holocaust survivors after 33 years: Data from an unbiased community sample. *American Journal of Psychiatry, 139*, 773–777.

Eitinger, L., & Strom, A. (1973). *Mortality and Morbidity After Excessive Stress: A Follow-up Investigation of Norwegian Concentration Camp Survivors.* New York: Humanities Press.

Eitinger, L. (1980). The Concentration Camp Syndrome and its Late sequelae. In, J. Dimsdale (Ed.), *Survivors, Victims and Perpetrators*. New York: Hemisphere.

Frankl, V.E. (1984). *Man's Search for Meaning: An Introduction to Logotherapy*. Boston, MA: Beacon Press.

George, L. (1990). Vulnerability and Social Factors. In Z. Harel, P. Ehrlich & R. Hubbard (Eds.). *The Vulnerable Aged: People, Policies and Programs*. New York: Springer.

Gill, A. (1988). *The Journey Back From Hell: An Oral History: Conversations with Holocaust Survivors*. New York: William Morrow & Co.

Harel, Z. & Noelker, L. (1982). Social integration, health, and choice: Their impact on the well-being of institutionalized aged, *Research on Aging*, 4, 97–111.

Harel, Z. & Deimling, G. (1984). Social resources and mental health: An empirical refinement, *Journal of Gerontology*, 39, 747–752.

Harel, Z., Kahana, B., & Kahana, E. (1988). Psychological well-being among Holocaust survivors and immigrants in Israel. *Journal of Traumatic Stress Studies, 1*, 4, 413–428.

Herman, J.L. (1997). *Trauma and Recovery*. New York: Basic Books.

Kahana, B., Harel, Z., & Kahana, E. (1988). Predictors of Psychological Well-being Among Survivors of the Holocaust. In J. Wilson, Z. Harel, & B. Kahana (Eds.), *Human Adaptation to Extreme Stress: From the Holocaust to Vietnam*, (pp.171–192). New York: Plenum.

Kahana, B., Harel, Z., & Kahana, E. (1989). Clinical and Gerontological Issues Facing Survivors of Holocaust. In P. Marcus & A. Rosenberg (Eds.). *Healing Their Wounds: Psychotherapy with Holocaust Survivors and Their Families*, (pp.197–212). New York: Praeger Publishers.

Kahana, B., Kahana, E., Harel, Z., Kelly, K., Monaghan, P., & Holland, L (1997). A Framework for Understanding the Chronic Stresses of Holocaust survivors. In M. Gottlieb (Ed.). *Coping with Chronic Stress*, (pp. 315–342). New York: Plenum Press Publishing Company.

Kobasa, S.C., Maddi, S.R., Kahn, S. (1982). Hardiness and health: A prospective study. *Journal of Personality & Social Psychology*, 42 (1), 168–177.

Krell, R. & Sherman, M.I. (Eds.) (1997). *Medical and Psychological Effects of Concentration Camps on Holocaust Survivors*. New Brunswick, NJ: Transaction Publishers.

Krystal, H. (1968). *Massive Psychic Trauma*. New York: International Universities Press.

Kuch, K., & Cox, B. (1992). Symptoms of PTSD in 124 survivors of the Holocaust. *American Journal of Psychiatry*, 149, 337–340.

Landau, R. & Litwen, H. (2000). The effects of extreme early stress in very old age, *Journal of Traumatic Stress*, 13 (3), 473–487.

Lavie, P. (2001). Current concepts: Sleep disturbances in the wake of traumatic events. *New England Journal of Medicine, 345, 25*, 1825–1832.

Lawton, M.P. (1975). The Philadelphia Geriatric Morale Scale: A revision. *Journal of Gerontology, 30*, 85–89.

Lindy, J. Green, B. & Wilson, J. (1988). Vietnam: A Casebook. New York: Bruner Mazel.

Mangen, D.J. & Peterson, W.A., Eds. (1982). *Research Instruments in Social Gerontology*. Minneapolis: University of Minnesota Press.

Neiderland, W. (1981). The survivor syndrome: Further observations and dimensions. *Journal of American Psychoanalytic Association*, 29, 413–425.

Marcus, P.R., Rosenberg, A. (1988). A Philosophical Critique of the "Survivor Syndrome" and Some Implications for Treatment. In Randolph L. Braham (Ed.), *The Psychological Perspectives of the Holocaust and of Its Aftermath, (pp)*. Social Science Monographs.

Orwid, M., Domagalska, K., & Pietruzewski, K. (1995). The psychosocial effects of the Holocaust on Jewish survivors living in Poland. *Psychiatria-Polska, 29*, 3, 29–48.

Rappaport, E. (1968). Beyond traumatic neurosis: A psychoanalytic study of late reactions to concentration camp trauma. *International Journal of Psycho-Analysis, 49*(4), 719–731.

Sadavoy, J. (1997). A review of the late-life effects of prior psychological trauma. *American Journal of Geriatric Psychiatry*, 5, 287–301.

Tornstam, L. (1992). The quo vadis of gerontology: On the scientific paradigm of Gerontology, *The Gerontologist*, 32(3), 318–326.

Yehuda, R., Elkin, A., Binder-Brynes, K., Kahana, B., Southwick, S.M., Schmeidler, J., & Giller, E.L., Jr. (1996). Dissociation in aging Holocaust survivors, *American Journal of Psychiatry*, 153(7), 935–940.

7

Social Resources and Psychological Well-Being

There has been considerable interest in the gerontological literature concerning the social resources and mental health of the aged. This interest has been stimulated by attempts in gerontological research to identify salient elements of "successful aging" and predictors of well-being, and by efforts to delineate dimensions of frailty and vulnerability among the aged (Harel, Noelker, & Blake, 1985; Kahana & Kahana, 1996; 2003). Cross-sectional studies on the well-being of the aged have shown that mental health is best predicted by health and functional status, socioeconomic status, and by social resources and/or social integration. There are consistent indications in the literature that higher levels of mental health and psychological well-being are associated with better health and functional status, higher socioeconomic status and higher economic resources (Bengtson, & Roberts, 1991; Hobfoll & Vaux, 1993). Psychological well-being has also been found to be associated with social interaction, social activity and social support (Harel & Deimling, 1984; Kahn, 1994).

While higher social resources are generally found to be associated with better mental health (Harel & Deimling, 1984), a common occurrence in the lives of older people is a decline in social roles, social contacts, and social relationships (Harel, et al., 1985; Antonucci, 1990). There has been, however, a controversy concerning the impact that declining involvement in social roles and social networks have for the psychological well-being of the aged. This controversy is reflected in competing theoretical formulations in the social psychological literature, in differences in the conceptual approaches employed in diverse studies of adjustment to aging, and in efforts to identify predictors of well-being among the aged (Larson, 1978; Antonucci, 1990).

Even though there has been an increased interest in the role and importance of social supports for persons during their advanced years of life, there have been few attempts to investigate the relative importance of social affiliations, social interaction, social support and self-disclosure for the psychological well-being of aged victims of extreme stress. The buffering effects of social supports on Holocaust survivors have been largely suggested by clinical observations (Davidson, 1979). To the extent that extreme stress places individuals at special risks for adverse mental health consequence, there is reason to expect that social resources should be particularly important as predictors of psychological well-being among survivors of traumatic experiences. In order to advance our theoretical formulations in social gerontology, there is a need for more empirical investigations on the importance of social resource variables for the psychological well-being of the aged who have experienced extreme stress.

Empirical evidence indicates that social support generally has a positive effect on the older people's functioning and psychological well-being (Kahn, 1994). Research shows that greater support received by the individual in the form of a close relationship with family members, friends, acquaintances, co-workers, and the larger community decreases the likelihood that the individual will experience stress or illness, which in turn may contribute to higher levels of well-being (Dean & Lin, 1977). There may be alternative processes promoting positive effects of social support on outcomes. Social support may act as an antecedent to psychological well-being or act as a buffer that reduces the effects of the undesirable experience.

The role that social interaction (visiting, phone calls, and going places) with family members and friends has in determining the mental health and well-being of the elderly is less clear. It is also suggested that informal activity, which involves social interactions, promotes life satisfaction because these relationships provide the role supports and opportunities necessary for maintaining an individual's self-esteem and self-concept (Rosow, 1967, Gottlieb, 1997). Mental health may also be enhanced by the perception that interpersonal resources are available to help meet needs evoked by stressful events (Ben-Sira, 1985; Krause, 1987).

Social networks that reflect potential availability of social supports can also exert a positive effect on reducing physical health symptoms subsequent to trauma. They may do so by buffering the effect of increased levels of stress (Cohen & Wills, 1985; Krause, 1987). There are indications that specific types of social support (e.g., emotional support, tangible help) buffer the impact of specific types of stressors (e.g., death of close family member, crime, and family crises) (Cohen & Wills, 1985; Krause, 1987). Research also indicates that giving assistance to others (Kahana, Harel, & Kahana, 1988) benefits the individual psychologically in terms of enhanced competence and self esteem (Midlarsky, Kahana, Corley, Schonbar, & Nemeroff, 1999).

Evidence is continuing to accumulate regarding the benefits of both direct and indirect effects of social networks on illness symptoms. These effects are not necessarily due to the amount of social contact or the quantity of social relationships, but may result from perceptions of availability of a supportive network that reduces feelings of isolation. (Kahana, Kahana, Harel, Kelly, Monaghan, & Holland, 1997).

It is important to note that social networks cannot be viewed as inherently or consistently supportive. Social networks may be, in some instances, not only unsupportive but may also serve as sources of stress to older persons, particularly when support is excessive and threatens autonomy of the recipient (Agich, 2003).

There have been few studies, which systematically investigated patterns of social interaction and social support and their relative importance for the mental health and/or psychological well-being of extreme stress victims. There is some evidence to indicate that greater social support is associated with better mental health among survivors of extreme stress (Elder & Clipp, 1988; Kahana et al., 1988; Harel, Kahana, & Kahana, 1988). In summary, it may be concluded that better social resources may be associated with better mental and physical health in the aged who experienced stressful life events (Pearlin & Schooler, 1978). Losses in social resources, and especially losses of family and close friends can also serve as serious stressors in the lives of the aged. Such social losses become more common as older persons reach old age (Kahana & Kahana, 1996; Kahana, 2001).

SOCIAL RESOURCES AND PSYCHOLOGICAL WELL-BEING OF HOLOCAUST SURVIVORS

The value of available social resources and social support in buffering the impact of stressful life situations has been extensively documented in the behavioral and social science literature as well as in the more applied fields of health and social welfare (Cobb, 1976; Levy & Pescosolido, 2002). In the field of gerontology, evidence about protection offered by diverse social supports against stress have also been amply documented, indicating benefits for the aged in terms of better physical health, mental health and psychological well-being (George, 1990; Harel, 1988).

Our present study explored differences in social resources and their relative importance as predictors of psychological well being among survivors of the Holocaust and comparison groups of European immigrants to the U.S. and to Israel as discussed in our previous chapters. Survivors came to the U.S. and Israel following World War II, while the comparison groups arrived in the U.S. and Israel prior to the war. The two groups differed in the experience of the Holocaust and date of immigration to their respective countries of immigration. One of the important objectives of this research was to examine differences in social resources and the value of social support for the psychological well-being of aging survivors of the Holocaust and members of the comparison groups. This focus exemplifies our interest in exploring not only the pathological consequences and the scars caused by the Holocaust, but to also ascertain the factors that are likely to reduce these adverse consequences and aid in the psychosocial adjustment of survivors to the post-stress conventional life.

MEASUREMENT OF SOCIAL RESOURCES

We aimed to move beyond earlier consideration of this variable as a single construct. In our prior research on social resources and mental health (Harel & Deimling, 1984), a factor analysis of the social resource measures yielded a differentiation between social affiliations, social interaction and social support, and the perceived adequacy of social resources. Another study, which examined the relationship between social resources and mortality, differentiated between three components: roles and attachments, social interaction, and social support (Blazer, 1982).

Recognition of the multidimensional nature of the term social resources, represents a significant conceptual and methodological refinement and should prove to be useful in stimulating future research in these areas. The present study of Holocaust survivors also differentiates between social networks, social interaction, and self disclosure—the latter variable being important for marshalling social support. Social support is more likely to be forthcoming to those able and willing to disclose the problem (Pennebaker, 1995). Our research examined the extent to which these social resource dimensions are of importance for the psychological well-being of Holocaust survivors and members of the comparison groups.

Four social resource variables were employed in this research. These included: a) social network: being married, having children, having brothers/sisters, and having relatives; b) social interaction: going places with, visiting, making phone calls, discussing, and confiding; c) self-disclosure: talking about every day issues, important issues, sex, finances and the Holocaust and d) affective and instrumental social support received and given. Higher scores indicate more interaction, more self disclosure, and more support given or received. Psychological well-being (morale) in this research was measured by the Philadelphia Geriatric Center (PGC) Morale Scale (Lawton, 1975).

Two sets of research questions were addressed in this research. The first question relates to the differences in social network, social interaction, self-disclosure and social support between survivors of the Holocaust and members of the comparison groups who arrived in the U.S. and Israel from the same countries prior to World War II. It may be expected that survivors would have a more restricted social network, more limited social interaction and social support and to be less likely to share with others concerns, ideas and feelings. These expectations are based on observations from the Holocaust literature (Chodoff, 1966) which suggest that the social world of Holocaust survivors is more constricted. The second set of questions relates to the importance of the social resource variables in predicting morale in both groups. Based on observations from the Holocaust literature (Danieli, 1982; Steinitz, 1982), it may be expected that the social interactions of Holocaust survivors would be more problematic and their support networks more limited. Consequently, absence of support would adversely affect their psychological well-being. Since there have been few previous studies focusing on social network, social interaction, self disclosure and social support among elderly Holocaust survivors and the role of social support on their psychological well-being, this research is aimed to provide answers to these questions, as indicated in Table 1.

COMPARING U.S. SURVIVORS AND IMMIGRANTS ON SOCIAL RESOURCE VARIABLES

Table 1 summarizes differences and similarities between survivors and immigrants related to social networks, supports, and self-disclosure. We have noted in our chapter on stress exposure that survivors in both the U.S. and Israel had lower morale than members of the comparison groups of immigrants. The comparison of survivors and immigrants on social network reveals that survivors in the U.S. were more likely to be married and had higher average number of children. Respondents in the immigrant group had somewhat higher number of relatives; however, the difference was not significant. In Israel, survivors had a significantly lower average number of children than immigrants, but there were no significant differences on other social network variables.

As indicated in Table 1, there were no differences noted between survivors and immigrants in social interaction in either the United States or Israel. The extent of visiting, phone calls and discussing issues was similar

Table 1. Morale and Social Resources

		Survivors		Immigrants		
		Mean	Std Dev	Mean	Std Dev	F Value
MORALE	U.S.	8.17	.03	10.48	2.40	57.01**
	Israel	9.32	3.91	10.99	3.56	17.03**
SOCIAL AFFILIATIONS						
Marital Status	U.S.	1.81	.39	1.69	.46	6.49**
	Israel	1.80	.40	1.76	.60	.42
# of Children	U.S.	2.30	1.07	1.92	1.28	8.09**
	Israel	1.73	1.04	2.16	1.01	14.79**
# of Brothers & Sisters	U.S.	1.39	1.61	1.08	1.14	3.65
	Israel	1.62	1.09	1.89	1.46	.59
# of Other Relatives	U.S.	3.77	4.55	4.23	4.75	.76
	Israel	5.08	5.89	6.78	6.60	2.07
SOCIAL INTERACTION						
Go places	U.S	7.74	2.75	7.79	2.59	.03
	Israel	6.69	3.02	6.57	2.75	.15
Visiting	U.S.	9.53	2.82	8.90	2.97	3.58
	Israel	8.90	2.77	9.14	2.60	.64
Phone calls	U.S.	12.12	2.61	11.83	3.01	.78
	Israel	11.42	2.69	1.53	2.84	.13
Discussion	U.S.	13.86	3.33	13.47	3.67	.95
	Israel	13.56	3.90	13.62	3.06	.03
Confiding	U.S.	1.04	.20	1.06	.25	.82
	Israel	1.13	.33	1.18	.38	2.14
SELF DISCLOSURE						
Everyday Issues	U.S.	13.60	3.91	12.79	3.30	3.46
	Israel	14.94	4.63	14.87	4.36	.02
Important Issues	U.S.	13.62	4.08	12.90	3.50	2.49
	Israel	14.46	4.58	14.17	4.01	.35
Sexual Issues	U.S.	7.16	2.21	6.92	2.23	.83
	Israel	7.44	2.75	7.36	2.66	.06
Financial Issues	U.S.	11.69	2.96	10.92	2.67	5.41*
	Israel	11.20	3.47	10.88	3.33	.70
SOCIAL SUPPORT-GIVEN						
Well being	U.S.	12.43	2.03	11.96	2.24	2.87
	Israel	10.04	1.53	9.60	2.34	0.61
Ideas	U.S.	10.53	2.19	10.43	1.92	0.13
	Israel	9.64	1.34	8.82	2.04	2.87
Transportation	U.S.	7.79	1.69	7.52	1.48	1.42
	Israel	6.85	0.98	7.12	1.94	0.49
Shopping	U.S.	8.09	1.66	7.47	1.46	8.72**
	Israel	7.89	1.11	7.65	1.44	0.36
Repairs	U.S.	7.31	1.60	6.41	0.43	29.41**
	Israel	7.02	1.09	6.82	1.45	0.26

Table 1. (*Cont.*)

		Survivors		Immigrants		
		Mean	Std Dev	Mean	Std Dev	F Value
Cooking	U.S.	7.56	1.71	6.98	1.16	8.96**
	Israel	7.68	1.01	6.95	1.41	4.27**
Finances	U.S.	8.14	1.85	7.57	1.53	6.40*
	Israel	7.70	1.05	7.27	1.30	1.48
Illness	U.S.	8.43	2.21	7.38	1.75	17.14**
	Israel	8.53	1.17	7.46	1.55	7.06**
SOCIAL SUPPORT RECEIVED						
Well being	U.S.	11.24	2.31	10.85	2.39	0.73
	Israel	8.69	2.30	8.50	2.39	0.49
Ideas	U.S.	10.20	2.11	9.65	1.91	2.07
	Israel	8.98	2.26	8.82	2.27	0.34
Transportation	U.S.	7.82	1.81	7.49	1.53	0.91
	Israel	6.72	1.09	6.78	1.08	0.22
Shopping	U.S.	7.65	1.44	7.32	1.07	1.31
	Israel	6.84	0.97	6.82	1.03	0.03
Repairs	U.S.	8.05	1.48	7.51	1.15	5.58*
	Israel	7.21	1.27	7.10	1.23	0.60
Cooking	U.S.	7.58	1.18	7.49	0.92	0.16
	Israel	6.86	1.05	6.87	1.25	0.01
Finances	U.S.	7.00	0.89	6.74	0.95	1.49
	Israel	6.58	0.89	6.56	0.94	0.01
Illness	U.S.	8.62	2.05	8.29	2.29	0.61
	Israel	7.38	1.57	7.25	1.70	0.45

*p = .05; **p = .01;

in the four groups. In terms of self-disclosure, survivors were somewhat more likely than members of the comparison groups to share concerns with their children, family members, friends and co-workers. The discussion of finances was significantly more frequent among survivors in Israel. Also, survivors were more likely to talk with others about the Holocaust, which is not unexpected.

There were a number of significant differences found between the two groups in the U.S. in giving support. Survivors living in the U.S. were more likely than members of the immigrant group to provide assistance to others with shopping, repairs, cooking, and finances and more likely to offer assistance in times of illness. These data suggests the notion of altruistic acts among persons who have endured extreme trauma (Midlarsky, et al., 1999).

Survivors were also slightly more likely to offer assistance with shopping, repairs and finances, to listen to ideas of others and to show more concern for the well being of their children, family members and friends. There were only some slight differences found between the two groups in offering of assistance in Israel. Survivors were significantly more likely than members of the immigrant group to give assistance in times of illness and assistance with cooking.

There were also some differences found between the two groups in receiving attention and assistance with survivors reporting receiving more, even though the differences were not significant. There were also some differences found between the two groups in receiving attention and assistance. Survivors were more likely than members of the comparison group to receive assistance with repairs, to get help in times of illness, to have others be concerned about their well-being and to have their ideas listened to.

These findings clearly indicate that in terms of social network, social interaction, self-disclosure and social support, aging survivors of the Holocaust in the U.S. and Israel are doing as well and in some instances better than members of the comparison group. These results are clearly contrary to the expectations based on early Holocaust literature (Danieli, 1982; Krystal, 1968). Our results indicate that survivors developed meaningful social networks, and utilized their social networks to engage in social interaction, to share their concerns and ideas with others and to develop supportive relationships to a somewhat greater extent than members of the immigrant groups. These findings suggest that survivors engaged in deliberate efforts to be involved with others and to regain social contact as much us possible. Contrary to some of the portrayals in the Holocaust literature (Chodoff, 1966; Danieli, 1982; Steinitz, 1982), survivors had to overcome indifference and misunderstanding in their respective social environments to actively pursue and develop meaningful networks of social support. Survivors' accomplishments in these area are noteworthy and are indicative of deliberate efforts reflective of other active coping patterns and social achievements.

SOCIAL RESOURCES AND PSYCHOLOGICAL WELL-BEING

The importance of social networks, social interaction, self-disclosure, and social support for the prediction of morale among survivors and immigrants are summarized in Table 2.

Consideration of the relationship between social resources and morale reveals that those who are married and have children and relatives are generally better off than others. Interestingly, having brothers or sisters has little impact on psychological well-being in either group. The data on social interaction in our research followed the general patterns found in the gerontological literature, indicating that those who have higher interaction

Table 2. Association of Social Resources and Morale

SOCIAL RESOURCES	U.S. sample		Israel sample	
	Survivors	Immigrants	Survivors	Immigrants
SOCIAL AFFILIATIONS				
Marital Status	.121	.156	.325**	.137
# of Children	.021	.155	.177	.108
Brothers & Sisters	−.028	−.050	−.009	.022
Relatives	.093	.109	.015	.083
SOCIAL INTERACTION				
Going Places	.006	.036	.095	.137
Visiting	−.009	−.084	.060	.107
Phone Calls	.084	−.058	.130	.038
Attention	.041	.116	.228*	.195*
Confiding	.104	.108	.001	.080
SELF DISCLOSURE				
Everyday Issues	−.056	.021	.340**	.241**
Important Issues	−.061	.105	.247**	.213*
Sexual Issues	.095	.133	.276**	.092
Financial Issues	.114	.002	.114	.164
SOCIAL SUPPORT-Given				
Well Being	.020	.067	.032	.112
Ideas	−.046	.015	.118	.116
Transportation	.107	.017	.039	.072
Shopping	.131	−.040	.003	−.026
Repairs	.032	.017	.058	.081
Cooking	.095	−.142	.025	−.058
Finances	.010	.078	−.049	.089
Illness	.264**	.131	.072	.010
SOCIAL SUPPORT-Received				
Well Being	−.099	−.015	.084	.141
Ideas	−.096	−.073	.168	.146
Transportation	−.032	−.110	.000	−.199*
Shopping	.023	−.015	.062	−.009
Repairs	.044	−.102	−.125	−.145
Cooking	.041	−.016	.082	.069
Finances	−.039	−.206*	−.004	−.006
Illness	−.087	−.087	−.001	−.024

*p = .05; **p = .01

with others have slightly higher psychological well-being (Larson, 1978). Of the social interaction variables, however, only self-disclosure in the form of discussion with others was significant in predicting morale for survivors in Israel. Among Israeli immigrants this association also approximated significance.

The review of data on self-disclosure also confirmed general findings from the gerontological literature that those who share everyday and important matters and readily talk with others about sex and finances are likely to have higher morale. Alternatively, it may be argued that those with high morale may be in a better position to self-disclose their situation. Interestingly, being a receiver of support did not enhance morale. Those receiving more assistance are portrayed with lower psychological well-being. Conversely, giving attention and assistance was found to be associated with better psychological well-being. These results support previous findings in the gerontological literature that being a recipient of support undermines self-esteem whereas being a provider of support to others enhances it (Midlarsky & Kahana, 1994).

AIDING THE SOCIAL ADJUSTMENT OF SURVIVORS
OF EXTREME STRESS

The purpose of this chapter was to provide a better understanding of the ways in which older survivors of extreme stress may use social resources to cope with their aging experiences, and derive implications for future research and practice efforts, based on the data obtained. Sensitivity is a prerequisite in research and work with all groups of elderly. It is even more important for the professionals who conduct research with older adults who are coping with consequences of extreme stress experienced earlier in their life. It is important that both research and practice with survivors of extreme stress not be based on faulty assumptions such as regarding social functioning of Holocaust survivors relative to others who did not share their traumatic experiences.

There is a clear indication in our data that the availability of social support and communication with members of one's primary group (i.e. spouse, children and other family members) and friends are indeed important contributors toward higher levels of psychological well-being. Survivors have made many efforts in their new environments to reconstruct social neworks and, in fact, possess similar or greater resources than persons of similar socio-cultural background who have not experienced the horrors of the Holocaust. This observation is supported by low divorce rates and relatively large families of procreation among survivors. Furthermore, survivors are actively engaged in social interactions and social support with their family members and friends. These relationships and exchanges contribute to their psychological well-being in similar ways to that of other cross-sections of older persons. These findings once again underscore that the results of studies conducted exclusively with those samples seeking mental health services cannot be generalized to the entire survivor population. Such studies have led to misconceptions and misleading generalizations about the entire population of Holocaust survivors.

Data from studies of nonclinical populations of Holocaust survivors underscore the importance of considering social resources as well as psychological problems of survivors of extreme stress. It is important to employ conceptual approaches anchored in the social and behavioral sciences in order to ascertain the range of personal characteristics and resources as well as the social and environmental factors, which may aid or hinder the adjustment of Holocaust survivors. In the absence of conceptual sophistication and methodological rigor faulty conclusions are derived which in turn serve to further disadvantage survivors of extreme stress.

REFERENCES

Agich, G. (2003). *Dependence and Autonomy in Old Age: An Ethical Framework for Long-Term Care.* New York: Cambridge University Press.

Antonucci, T. (1990). Social supports and social relationships. In R. Binstock & L. George (Eds.), *Handbook of Aging and the Social Sciences, 3rd Edition* (pp. 205–227). New York: Academic Press.

Bengtson, V. & Roberts, R. (1991). Intergenerational solidarity in aging families: An example of formal theory construction. *Journal of Marriage and the Family*, 53, 856–870.

Ben-Sira, Z. (1985). Potency: A stress-buffering link in the coping-stress-disease relationship, *Social Science and Medicine*, 21(4), 397–406.

Blazer, D. (1982). Social support and mortality in an elderly community population, *American Journal of Epidemiology*, 115, 684–694.

Cassel, J. (1976). The contribution of the social environment to host resistance, American *Journal of Epidemiology*, 104, 107–123.

Chodoff, P. (1966). Effects of Extreme Coercive and Oppressive Forces: Brainwashing and Concentration Camps. In S. Arieti (Ed.), *American Handbook of Psychiatry, III.* New York: Basic Books, pp. 384–405.

Cobb, S. (1976). Social support as a moderator of life stress, *Psychosomatic Medicine*, 38, 300–314.

Cohen, S. & Wills, T.A. (1985). Stress, social support, and the buffering hypothesis. *Psychological Bulletin*, 982, 310–357.

Danieli, Y. (1982). Families of Survivors of the Nazi Holocaust: Some Short and Long Term Effects. In C.D. Spielberger, I.G. Sarason & N. A. Milgram (Eds.). *Stress and Anxiety*. Washington, D.C.: Hemisphere Publishing, 405–421.

Dean, A. & Lin, N. (1977). The stress-buffering role of social support, *Journal of Nervous and Mental Disease*, 165, 403–417.

Elder, G. & Clip, E. (1988). Combat Experience, Comradeship, and Psychological Health. In J. P. Wilson, Z. Harel and B. Kahana (Eds.), *Human Adaptation to Extreme Stress: From the Holocaust to Vietnam.* New York: Plenum.

George, L. (1990). Vulnerability and Social Factors. In Z. Harel, P. Ehrlich & R. Hubbard (Eds.). *Vulnerable Aged: People, Policies and Programs.* New York: Springer.

Gottlieb, B.H. (1997). *Coping with Chronic Stress.* New York: Plenum Press.

Harel, Z. (1988). Coping with extreme stress and aging, *Social Casework*, (November, 1988), 575–583.

Harel, Z. & Deimling, G. (1984). Social resources and mental health: An empirical refinement. *Journal of Gerontology*, 39, 747–752.

Harel, Z., Kahana, B., & Kahana, E. (1988). Predictors of psychological well-being among Holocaust survivors and immigrants in Israel, *Journal of Traumatic Stress*, 1(4), 413–428.

Harel, Z., Noelker, L. & Blake B. (1985). Planning Services for the Aged: Theoretical and Empirical Perspectives, *Gerontologist*, 25, 644–9.

Hobfoll, S. & Vaux, A. (1993). Social support: Social resources and social context. In L. Goldberger & S. Breznitz (Eds.), *Handbook of Stress: Theoretical and Clinical Aspects, 2nd Edition* (pp. 685–705). New York: Free Press.

Kahana, E. & Kahana, B. (1996). Conceptual and empirical advances in understanding aging well through proactive adaptation. In V. Bengtson (Ed.). *Adulthood and Aging: Research on Continuities and Discontinuities* (pp. 18–40). New York: Springer.

Kahana, E. (2001). Loss. In G. Maddox (Ed.), *Encyclopedia of Aging, 3rd Edition* (pp. 636–638). New York: Springer.

Kahana, E. & Kahana, B. (2003). Contextualizing Successful Aging: New Directions in Age-Old Search. In R. Settersten, Jr. (Ed.), *Invitation to the Life Course: A New Look at Old Age*, (pp. 225–255). Amityville, NY: Baywood Publishing Company.

Kahana, B., Kahana, E., Harel, Z., Kelly, K., Monaghan, P., & Holland, L. (1997). A Framework for Understanding the Chronic Stress of Holocaust Survivors. In M. Gottlieb (Ed.), Coping with Chronic Stress (pp. 315–342). New York, NY: Plenum Publishing Co.

Kahana, B., Harel, Z. & Kahana, E. (1988). Predictors of Psychological Well-Being Among survivors of the Holocaust. In J. P. Wilson, Z. Harel and B. Kahana (Eds.), *Human Adaptation to Extreme Stress: From the Holocaust to Vietnam*, (171–192). New York: Plenum.

Kahn, R. (1994). Social support: Content, causes, and consequences. In R. Abeles, H. Gift & M. Ory (Eds.), *Aging and Quality of Life* (pp. 163–184). New York: Springer.

Krause N. (1987). Chronic financial strain, social support, and depressive symptoms among older adults, *Psychology & Aging*, 22, 185–192.

Krystal, H. (1968). Studies of concentration camp Survivors. In H. Krystal (Ed.), *Massive Psychic Trauma*, (pp. 23–46). New York: International Universities Press.

Larson, R., (1978). Thirty years of research on the subjective well-being of older Americans, *Journal of Gerontology*, 33, 109–129.

Lawton, M. P. (1975). The Philadelphia Geriatric Center morale scale: A revision, *Journal of Gerontology*, 30 85–89.

Levy, J. & Pescosolido, B. (2002). *Advances in Medical Sociology, Volume 8: Social Networks and Health*. New York: JAI.

Midlarsky, E. & Kahana, E. (Eds.). (1994). *Altruism in Later Life*. Newbury Park, CA: Sage Publications.

Midlarsky, E., Kahana, E., Corley, R. Schonbar, R., Nemeroff, R. (1999). Altruistic moral judgment among older adults, *International Journal of Aging and Human Development*, 49(1), 27–41.

Pearlin, L.I. & Schooler, C. (1978). The structure of coping. *Journal of Health & Social Behavior*, 19(1),2–21.

Pennebaker, J.W. (1995). *Emotion, Disclosure & Health*. Washington, DC: American Psychological Association.

Rosow, J. (1967). *Social Integration of the Aged*. New York: The Free Press.

Steinitz L. Y. (1982). Psycho-social effects of the Holocaust on aging survivors and their families, *Journal of Gerontological Social Work*, 4(3/4), 145–152.

8

Predictors of Psychological Well-Being
A Multivariate Model

This chapter reviews predictors of psychological well-being among survivors of the Holocaust and immigrants of similar socio-cultural background living in the U.S. and Israel. Six independent variable groups that included socio demographic characteristics, socio economic status, health, stress, personal coping, and communication with significant social resources were employed in these analyses. The analyses included a comparison of survivors and immigrant groups on the independent variables, an examination of the bi-variate association between the independent variables and psychological well being (morale), and the identification of the best predictors of psychological well-being in multivariate regression analyses.

In this chapter, predictors of psychological well-being among survivors of the Holocaust and comparison groups of European immigrants in the U.S. and to Israel are reviewed and discussed. As indicated throughout this book, survivors came to Israel and the U.S. following World War II, while members of the comparison groups arrived at the U.S. and Israel prior to the war. The two groups differed in the experience of the Holocaust and date of immigration to the U.S. and Israel. This study affords the opportunity to examine the differences in psychological well-being between survivors and individuals who have not experienced the Holocaust. In addition, this research assessed predictors of psychological well-being in both groups.

This research employs behavioral and social science perspectives in considering sequelae of massive psychic trauma (Kahana & Kahana, 2001). One of the primary objectives of this research is to examine the importance of personal characteristics (socio-demographic and socio-economic status and health), cumulative and recent life stresses, and post-war adaptation as they have impacted on the psychological well-being of aging survivors of the Holocaust and the comparison groups of immigrants. The analyses in this chapter represent an effort to understand the importance of social and psychological factors in the lives of survivors and to ascertain the importance of these variables among survivors as compared with persons of similar background who have not experienced the Holocaust.

Recent literature and research on predictors of mental health among survivors point toward four variable groups which are likely to affect the long term adaptation and well-being among victims of extreme stress. These variable groups include: 1) stress factors (nature and duration of stress experiences); 2) current socio-demographic and socio-economic status; 3) current health status; and 4) current modes of coping with conventional life and survivorship experiences (Kahana, Harel & Kahana, 1988). Although, to date, research, has not focused on the potential influence of post-Holocaust coping and adaptation patterns in mitigating negative consequences of stress, there are compelling arguments for considering ongoing adaptive efforts. The broad questions of human adaptation and adjustment have long been central to theoretical formulations dealing with personality, social behavior, and mental health (Gottlieb, 1997; Lazarus & Folkman, 1984).

Social and behavioral scientists have long been intrigued by the human capacity to endure and rebound from extreme stress. Reliance on conceptual approaches, which incorporate behavioral, and social science perspectives is necessary in attempts to understand the ways in which survivors adjusted to the demands and challenges in the post-war years. This chapter goes beyond the notion that trauma causes long-range irreparable damage. It explores not only the pathological consequences and the scars caused by the Holocaust, but also ascertains the factors, which are likely to reduce these adverse consequences and promote the psychosocial adjustment of survivors in the post war years.

CONCEPTUAL APPROACH AND MEASUREMENT

In considering long term post-traumatic adaptation of survivors of extreme trauma, it is useful to integrate concepts from both the gerontological and trauma literatures. The present research sought to study psychological well-being and predictors of psychological well-being among a broad and diverse cross-section of Holocaust survivors and comparison groups of immigrants in two countries; the United States and Israel. Psychological well-being is the major outcome variable measured by the Philadelphia Geriatric Center (PGC) Morale Scale (Lawton, 1975). Morale has been frequently used in gerontological research for the assessment of psychological well-being among the aged. This measure is seen as a useful indicator of positive adjustment in later years (Larson, 1978; Lawton, 1975). It consists of three factors.

In the selection of predictor variables two criteria were used. First, variables typically used in social gerontological research seeking to explain psychological well-being were included. Second, variables, which are considered as potentially mediating the effects of extreme stress on mental health, were selected. For these reasons this study included socio-demographic characteristics, socio-economic status and health variables, as well as stress variables, and personal coping and resource variables. These variables were seen as useful in an attempt to integrate conceptual approaches prevalent in social gerontological research with conceptual issues, which may be more salient to the understanding of the effects of stress experiences of survivors in the post-war years (Kahana, Harel, & Kahana, 1982).

Socio-demographic variables in this research included age, gender, marital status, work background, perceived income adequacy, and education before and after the war. Health measures reported included self-rated health and an inventory of illnesses (Blazer, 1978). These variables were selected because of the extensive empirical evidence indicating their importance for the prediction of psychological well-being among the aged (Harel, Noelker, & Blake, 1985; Larson, 1978) and because of the likelihood that these variables will reduce or exacerbate adverse stress consequences (Kahana, 1992).

Stress measures, in this research, include an inventory of life crises (Antonovsky, 1979), recent life events (Kahana, Fairchild & Kahana, 1982), and an inventory of personal and social concerns (Kahana, Harel & Kahana, 1982). These variables were included because studies of Holocaust survivors and stress research indicate adverse consequences of cumulative stress on psychological well-being among stress victims (Chodoff, 1966; Lazarus & Folkman, 1984).

Personal coping and resource variables, which have been found to moderate deleterious effects of stress on psychological well-being, were also included in this research (Lazarus, & Folkman 1984). Personal coping resources would be reflected in a stronger achievement orientation, higher locus of control, greater reliance on instrumental coping, lower reliance on emotional coping, and better communication with family members and friends about salient aspects of everyday life. These variables were included because of converging evidence that present social and psychological adaptation is conducive to a higher level of psychological well-being among stress victims (Aldwin & Brustrom, 1997; Kahana, et. al., 1988; Lazarus & Folkman, 1984). Measures of personal resources and coping included: locus of control (Wrightsman, 1974), personality style (Friedman & Rosenman, 1974), coping style (Kahana, Kahana, Harel & Rosner, 1988; Shanan, 1989), and communication with significant social network members (Antonucci & Akiyama, 1987; Kahana, Harel & Kahana, 1988).

Two sets of working hypotheses were assessed in this chapter. The first relates to the differences between survivors of the Holocaust and members of the comparison group who arrived in the U.S. and Israel from the same countries prior to World War II. On the bases of findings from the Holocaust literature (Kahana & Kahana, 2001), it was expected that survivors would have lower morale compared with those in the comparison group. Because of the differences in the war-time experiences, it was expected that survivors would have more cumulative life stresses and higher personal and social concerns. This is based on the assumption that survivors not only experienced more stress but were also more likely to have been negatively affected by their Holocaust experiences and, therefore, would have a greater need to remain concerned since every new stress situation may be seen as a potential threat to them. These concerns may be perceived by survivors as endangering their own social and psychological well being and that of their significant others. Survivors are also more likely to perceive the probability of the recurrence of dangers, which they have experienced and observed during the war years (Gottlieb, 1997). To date, there have been few studies, which systematically compared personal, economic, political and social concerns of survivors with comparison groups of similar socio-cultural background who have not experienced the Holocaust. In one such study conducted in Montreal (Weinfeld, Sigal & Eaton, 1981) no significant differences were found between survivors and a control group of immigrants on perception of anti-Semitism, level of economic and political satisfaction, and probability of emigration.

It was expected, however, that survivors as a group would score higher on the "active coping traits" of the Framingham Scale and would also have higher locus of control. This was based on the assumption that these traits enabled survivors to endure the dangers and difficulties to which they were exposed during the war years. It was also expected that survivors, as a group, would portray more active coping strategies. This is based on the assumption that survivors were more frequently called upon to practice various coping skills during the war and in the post-war years. It was expected that survivors would have higher levels of communication with their spouses, children and other family members because of the importance they attributed to their families (Weinfeld, Segal & Eaton, 1981).

The review of gerontological literature indicates that health and functional status, along with income adequacy, socio-economic status and social resources are frequently found to be significant predictors of well-being among the aged (Harel & Deimling, 1984; Larson, 1978; Palmore, 1979). It was expected that these variables would have similar importance in the prediction of psychological well-being among survivors and among members of the comparison group. Therefore, it was hypothesized that being married, having higher perceived income adequacy and better health would be associated with higher psychological well-being in both groups. It was also expected that less stress, less concern, instrumental coping, and more communication would also be associated with higher psychological well-being in both groups (Harel & Deimling, 984; Kahana, Harel & Kahana, 1982).

Most measures employed in this research have been extensively used in previous studies. A small number of measures (social concern and communication) were developed by the authors for this research (Kahana, Harel & Kahana, 1982). To assure the appropriateness of existing measures, as well as those developed by the authors for this study (Kahana et al., 1982), factor analyses were performed and reliability of each measure was ascertained. The results of the reliability testing yielded generally acceptable reliability scores ranging from the low sixties to the mid eighties.

The measures for socio-demographic and socio-economic status are the ones employed in gerontological research (Harel & Deimling, 1984). The self-rated health, and illness inventory were adapted from the OARS instrument (Blazer, 1978), a measure that has been extensively used in gerontological research. To ascertain cumulative and recent stressful experiences and concerns in the lives of the respondents several measures were employed. Two measures of life crises frequently employed in gerontological research were included in this research: a cumulative life crisis history (Antonovsky, 1979); and the impact of life changes based on the Elderly Care Research Center (ECRC) Recent Life Event Scale (Kahana, Fairchild & Kahana, 1982).

The two measures, Antonovsky Life Crises History and the ECRC Recent Life Event Scale, were used to generate summative scores. The reliability testing of these measures yielded alpha coefficients in the sixties. A measure of social concern was specially developed by the authors and employed in this research. The Social Concern measure was subjected to a factor analysis and yielded two concern constructs, one reflecting concern about Jewish life including the State of Israel (war, rise of anti-Semitism, another Holocaust, threat to the State of Israel) and one reflecting more universal concerns (nuclear destruction, depression, economic security). The reliability testing of these measures yielded alpha coefficients in the seventies and eighties. Several measures of personal coping and resources were included in this research. These are Wrightsman's Locus of Control (Wrightsman, 1974), and the Framingham's Scale (Friedman & Rosenman 1974). Wrightsman Locus of Control measure, when subjected to factor analysis yielded two components, one more directly reflecting perceived locus of control and a second factor—not being resigned to fate Framingham's Scale yielded two factors: one referred to here as an "achievement" factor (hard driving, pressed for time, bossy, need to excel, eating quickly), and a second referred to here as a "hard working" factor (very pressed, work stays with me, work is demanding, uncertain how well one is doing).

Comparisons of personal coping resources reveal differential patterns for respondents living in the U.S. and those living in Israel on the two subscales of the Wrightsman locus of control measure. On the first factor, termed "locus of control," U.S. survivors and immigrants showed no differences, whereas on the second "not resigned" factor immigrants in the U.S. were found to be significantly less resigned. In Israel, immigrants showed significantly more internal locus of control on the first factor (locus of control) and slightly less resignation on the second factor (not resigned). It is possible that the extreme trauma endured by survivors in both countries played a role in altering their beliefs about controllability of life circumstances. With regard to the Framingham index's factor reflecting achievement orientation, survivors showed significantly higher achievement orientation in the U.S. On the factor denoting hard work, survivors scored higher in both countries, but differences were not statistically significant.

Survivors in both countries were more likely to endorse coping items on all three types of coping measured by the coping scale, included in this study (instrumental coping, emotional coping, and escapist coping) For the Israeli sample, these differences reach statistical significance on all three coping measures whereas in the U.S the differences are significant only for escape/avoidance oriented coping. These findings diverge from prior research that generally found people who engage in instrumental coping to be less likely to engage in affective or in escape/avoidance oriented coping strategies.(Kahana, Kahana, and Young, 1987). It is possible that survivors benefited from engaging in diverse modes of coping during the difficult years of the war. Such multiple coping responses may have served them well as they experienced multiple difficulties during the Holocaust.

A measure of coping, the ECRC Coping Scale, was also included in this research. The ECRC Coping Scale was subjected to a factor analysis, which yielded three constructs, instrumental coping, emotional coping, and avoidant/escapist coping. Subjecting the coping measures to reliability testing yielded alpha coefficients ranging from the mid fifties to the mid eighties. The communication measure included everyday concerns, important matters, concerns about sex and finances. The reference groups for communication included a spouse, children, grandchildren, other family members, friends and co-workers. Factor analyses indicated that data aggregation should be based on reference groups rather than on subject matter. Reliability testing of communication with the reference groups yielded alpha coefficients from the sixties to the eighties.

RESEARCH FINDINGS

Table 8 summarizes the descriptive data (means and standard deviations) on the variables included in our research for both groups and the results of the testing for the significance of the differences between the two groups, Holocaust survivors and immigrants in both the United States and Israel.

There were generally few differences between the survivor and immigrant respondents on socio-demographic (age, sex, marital status) and socio-economic status (occupational status income adequacy and education) in either one of the two countries. Significant differences were found on age (survivors being younger) in both countries and on marital status (more survivors were married) in the U.S. sample. On socio-economic variables, immigrant respondents attained higher educational status prior to WWII in both samples (survivors attaining about one year less). In the U.S. sample, members of the comparison group attained higher educational status also after the war and had a higher perceived income adequacy.

Not surprisingly, as indicated in the health chapter in this book, survivors rated their health to be significantly poorer than that of the immigrants, and also reported greater severity of illnesses than their immigrant counterparts in both countries. Survivors as a group reported significantly higher incidences of life crises (Antonovsky, 1979), than those in the immigrant group, in both countries and, in Israel, had also significantly higher incidents of recent life events. Regarding concerns with general and universal threats, both the U.S. and Israeli survivors reported significantly higher concerns (likelihood of war, another Holocaust, rise of anti-Semitism, threat to security of Israel). These findings, similar to those of a study conducted in Montreal (Weinfeld, Sigal & Eaton, 1981) may be explained by the harsher realities of Israeli life and greater importance attributed to the survival of the State of Israel and concerns for its security by survivors who were living in Israel.

Survivors were found to have slightly lower levels of locus of control in both countries. Concerning the "being resigned" factor, survivors were found to be (significantly) less resigned in Israel but more resigned in the U.S. These findings are in line with data we have reported earlier on the greater sense of isolation and mistrust experienced by survivors (Kahana et al., 1997). Survivors in Israel reported slightly higher levels of intensity on the two personality measures (Framingham first and second factors), indicating that they were more likely to be achievement oriented and to have a tendency to be more active and pressed for time than members of the comparison group, while in the U.S., the pattern was found to be reversed. Survivors were found to have engaged in higher levels of coping

Table 8. Correlates of Morale Among Survivors of the Holocaust and Immigrants
in the U.S. and Israel

	US SAMPLE		ISRAELI SAMPLE	
VARIABLES	SURVIVORS	IMMIGRANTS	SURVIVORS	IMMIGRANTS
SOCIO-DEMOGRAPHIC				
Age	−.04	−.18**	−.17*	−.06
Sex	−.21**	−.19**	−.17*	−.16*
Marital Status	.12	.16	.33**	.23**
SOCIO-ECONOMIC				
Work Background	.06	.17*	.11	.05
Income Adequacy	.33**	.02	.20**	.17**
Education before war	.20**	.09	.06	−.02
Education after war	.11	.17*	.12	.07
HEALTH				
Self rated Health	.27**	.22**	.35**	.27**
Illness Severity	−.42**	−.27**	−.26**	−.21**
STRESS & CONCERNS				
Antonovsky Life Crises	−.43**	−.15*	−.24**	−.16*
Recent Life Events	−.20**	−.09	−.09	−.04
Jewish Concerns	−.25**	−.03	−.18**	−.28
Universal Concerns	−.13*	−.30**	−.33**	−.13*
PERSONAL RESOURCES & COPING				
Wrightsman Locus of Control Subscale	.08	.03	.15*	.06
Wrightsman Not resigned to Future	.25**	.26**	.37**	.19**
Framingham Achievement	.13*	.11	.17*	.20**
Framingham Hard Work	.33**	.13*	.15*	.21*
ECRC Coping Scale				
Instrumental Coping	.14*	.18**	.14*	.18**
Emotional Coping	−.32**	−.12	−.33**	−.18**
Avoidant/Escapist Coping	−.36**	−.25**	−.16*	−.14*
COMMUNICATIONS				
With Spouse	.15*	.19**	.31**	.29**
With Children	−.12	−.07	.24**	.27**
With Grandchildren	−.01	−.18**	.09	.03
With Family	−.12	−.15*	.20	.03
With Friends	−.07	−.14*	.07	.08
With Coworkers	.13*	.08	.29**	.08

*p = .05; **p = .01

on all three types of coping measured by the coping scales included in this study (instrumental coping, emotional coping and escapist coping) in both countries.

These findings indicate that survivors, in comparison with individuals who have not experienced the Holocaust, are more likely to continue to portray the traits, which enabled them to endure the difficulties to which they were exposed to during the war years. It is notable that they were engaging in more diverse modes of coping than non-traumatized population. It is generally found that people engaging in instrumental coping are less likely to engage in affective or escapist coping (Kahana, Kahana, & Harel, 1997).

Survivors, in both countries, were found to have significantly higher levels of communication with their children and, in the U.S., significantly, higher levels of communication with their spouses. In communication with other reference groups the differences were small and insignificant.

Survivors were found to have lower morale than members of the comparison group in both countries, confirming other findings in which survivors are found to have poorer mental health and lower levels of psychological well-being than members of comparison groups (Hyer & Sohnle, 2001; Shmotkin & Lomrantz, 1998).

These findings indicate generally less difference between survivors and individuals of similar background who have not experienced the Holocaust on post war coping and adaptation than would be expected on the basis of the clinical studies of Holocaust survivors (Danieli, 1998). Our more postive portrayal of psychological functioning of survivors than those in earlier studies may be accounted for by our focus on non-clinical samples of survivors who did not actively seek mental health services.

The review of the correlation tables reveals that in both groups, survivors and immigrants, higher morale was found to be associated with being married, with male gender, and with younger age. The associations between gender and psychological well being were significant in all groups. Being married was significantly associated with morale in all groups but the U.S. survivors where the association approached but did not reach significance. Higher age was significantly associated with lower morale among immigrants in the U.S. and survivors in Israel.

All socio-economic variables were generally found to have positive association with morale. Working in higher level jobs was significantly associated with better psychological well being among immigrants in the U.S. Higher income adequacy was found to be significantly correlated with morale in both groups in Israel and among survivors in the U.S. Members of the immigrant group in the U.S. who achieved higher educational attainment after World War II and U.S. survivors who spend more years on education before the war were found to have significantly higher morale. These findings are consistent with data from gerontological research, which link social resources with psychological well-being (Harel & Deimling, 1984; Kasl, 1992). Better health and fewer illnesses were significantly correlated with higher morale for both survivors and immigrants living in both countries. These data confirm the importance of health, higher socio economic status, (younger) age, (married) marital status, and gender as correlates of morale, a finding similar to cross-sectional studies on predictors of well-being among the aged (Larson, 1978; Harel & Deimling, 1984).

Table 9. SURVIVORS OF THE HOLOCAUST IN THE U.S. PREDICTORS OF MORALE

	All Variables	Significant Variables		
MULTIPLE R	.72	.68		
R SQUARE .	.52	.46		
ADJUSTED R SQUARE	.41	.43		

VARIABLES	B	SE B	BETA	T	SIG T
Antonovsky-Life Crises	−.37	.08	−.31	−4.66	.001
Emotional Coping	−.23	.08	−.21	−3.02	.003
Resigned Coping	−.16	.05	−.21	−3.06	.003
Instrumental Coping	.09	.04	.16	2.83	.019
Education before war	.11	.04	−.19	3.09	.002
Communication coworkers	.15	.04	.15	2.24	.027
Universal concerns	.19	.07	.19	2.72	.007
Framingham hard work	.28	.14	.14	1.99	.049

IMMIGRANTS IN THE U.S.
PREDICTORS OF MORALE

	All Variables	Significant Variables		
MULTIPLE R	.58	.46		
R SQUARE	.33	.21		
ADJUSTED R SQUARE	.22	.18		

VARIABLES	B	SE B	BETA	T	SIG T
Resigned Coping	−.25	.06	−.36	−4.18	.001
Age	−.08	.03	−.34	−3.13	.002
Education Before War	−.12	.06	−.21	2.06	.042
Communication-Friends	.17	.08	.17	−2.11	.037
Health	.57	.28	.17	2.06	.042
Instrumental Coping	.06	.03	.17	−1.89	.060

Of the crises and concern variables, in general in all groups, experiencing life crises, negative recent life events, and being concerned about future adversities were associated with lower morale. In all groups, more life crises and universal concerns were associated with lower morale. Among survivors in Israel, also, recent life events and concerns about the future of Jews and Israel were associated with lower morale. Higher level of concern with future of Jews was also negatively associated with morale in both groups in Israel.

All personal coping resources, with the exception of locus of control among members of the comparison group, were significantly associated with high morale, though the associations ranged from limited to highly significant associations. Of the coping measures, as expected, higher level of instrumental coping had a significant association with higher morale while higher level of emotional coping and escapist coping were significantly associated with lower morale. Of the communication measures, higher level of communication with spouse and children were significantly associated with higher morale in both groups. Among survivors, communication with other family members and with co-workers was also positively associated with morale. Findings from the correlational analyses, again, indicate generally little difference between survivors and immigrants regarding the determinants of psychological well-being.

MULTIVARIATE ANALYSES

A two stage, multiple regression analysis was performed. First, all predictor variables were entered into the regression equation to ascertain the total explained variance. Second, variables which were not significant in the prediction of morale were excluded via a stepwise multiple regression procedure. The results of the regression analyses are presented first for the U.S. and, second, for Israel. In the first multiple regression analysis, when all predictor variables were entered, these accounted for 52 percent of explained variance in morale for the U.S. survivors.

In the stepwise multiple regression analysis, eight measures accounted for 46 percent of explained variance in morale among survivors in U.S. These included: three coping measures (lesser use of emotional and resigned coping and higher use of instrumental coping); fewer life crises and fewer universal concerns regarding life, better health; higher level of education before World War II, higher level of communication with co-workers, and a drive to work hard.

In the multiple regression analysis for the comparison group, when all predictor variables were entered, these accounted for 33 percent explained

Table 10. SURVIVORS OF THE HOLOCAUST IN ISRAEL PREDICTORS OF MORALE

	All Variables	Significant Variables			
MULTIPLE R	.75	.72			
R SQUARE .	.56	.52			
ADJUSTED R SQUARE	.53	.49			

VARIABLE	B	SE B	BETA	T	SIG T
Emotional Coping	−.34	.07	−.33	−5.08	.001
Marital Status	2.96	.62	.30	4.77	.001
Wrightsman not Resigned to Future	.83	.22	.24	3.77	.001
Health	1.05	.31	.22	3.42	.001
Concerns about future of Israel	−.18	.06	−.19	−2.76	.007
Communication coworkers	.22	.08	.17	2.63	.010
Antonovsky Life Crises	−.19	.08	−.15	2.33	.021
Instrumental Coping	.14	.06	.16	2.27	.025

IMMIGRANTS IN ISRAEL PREDICTORS OF MORALE

	All Variables	Significant Variables			
MULTIPLE R	.58	.46			
R SQUARE	.33	.21			
ADJUSTED R SQUARE	.22	.18			

VARIABLE	B	SE B	BETA	T	SIG T
Communication with Spouse	.19	.05	.29	3.71	.001
Emotional Coping	−.29	.09	−.29	−3.39	.001
Framingham Hard Work	−.75	.24	−.26	−3.16	.002
Health	1.17	.38	.25	3.08	.003
Instrumental Coping	.18	.06	.26	3.03	.003
Concerns Universal	−.14	.07	−.18	−2.14	.034

variance in morale. As indicated in the lower part of Table 10a, in the stepwise multiple regression analysis, among members of the comparison group, the following variables were significant and predicted 21 percent of explained variance in morale: two coping measures (lower resigned coping and higher instrumental coping); being younger, better health; lesser communication with friends; and higher level of education before the war.

In the first multiple regression analysis, when all predictor variables were entered, these accounted for 56 percent of explained variance in morale for the Israeli survivors.

In the stepwise multiple regression analysis, eight significant measures accounted for 52 percent of explained variance in morale among survivors. These included: two coping measures (lesser use of emotional coping and higher use of instrumental coping); fewer life crises and fewer concerns regarding life future; better health; being married; not being resigned to fate (higher internal locus of control); and higher level of communication with co-workers.

Findings from the multi-variate analyses, again, indicate generally greater similarity than difference between survivors and immigrants who have not experienced the Holocaust on factors that are significant predictors of psychological well-being in the post-war years in both the U.S. and Israel. Generally, instrumental coping, and better health are predictors of higher morale; while higher levels of stress and general concern and emotional and resigned coping are predictors of lower psychological well-being.

DISCUSSION

These findings clearly indicate that being married, better health and adequate income are important in the prediction of psychological well-being among both survivors and among immigrants who have not been exposed to the stresses of the Holocaust. Furthermore, there is an indication that better health and being married are not only found to be significant in the bi-variate association but also retain their significance in the multi-variate analyses as well.

These findings suggest that among survivors, as well as among those who have not experienced the Holocaust, better health, the support of a spouse, and income adequacy are among very important factors for psychological well-being in the advanced years of life. These data contribute, therefore, important evidence to the increasing body of gerontological literature regarding the universal importance of better health and functional status, adequate economic resources, and being married for better psychological well-being in advanced years of life (Larson, 1978).

The review of the data in this research on crises and concern variables, indicates that, in Israel, social concerns are pervasive and, the greater the concern, the lower the psychological well-being in both groups. Since life in Israel reflects an ongoing state of danger, it may not be surprising to find that constant concern for the future may lead to lower morale. In this regard, it is important to underscore the fact that both the survivors in this study, as well as members of the immigrant group, came to Israel from European countries where anti-Semitism was rampant and personal threats on Jewish life were frequent occurrences.

The continued threat to survival by the surrounding Arab countries, equally affect the psychological well-being of aging members of Israeli society. In addition, these data indicate some differences in the psychological well-being of the two groups. This is evidenced by the fact that among survivors, lower morale is more affected by higher cumulative life stress over the years, whereas in the comparison group greater universal concerns such as economic security play a greater importance. These data also indicate that personal coping and resources are significant predictors of psychological well-being. The most significant indications of the findings in this area are that a) reliance on emotional and resigned coping are conducive to lower psychological well-being, while b) instrumental coping contributes toward higher psychological well-being among both survivors and among members of the immigrant group.

There are also indications in the data that the availability of social support and communication with members of ones primary group (spouse, children, family members and friends), are indeed important contributors towards higher levels of psychological well-being in both groups. These data confirm the utility of employing conceptual approaches anchored in the behavioral and social sciences for the study of psychological well-being among survivors of the Holocaust, and possibly among other survivor populations of extreme stress. The data from this study clearly indicate that current states of psychological well-being among survivors are affected by recent states of health and functional status, cumulative life experiences, coping, adaptation and social support in ways similar to those found in cross-sectional studies of other populations of older persons.

Finally, it is important to underscore that our findings point to fewer differences between Holocaust survivors and immigrants than one would expect. The findings of more limited adverse sequelae among survivors in our study than those reported in prior work may be due to our respondents being randomly selected individuals rather than clinical populations of help seekers for mental health problems.

REFERENCES

Aldwin, L.M., Brustrom. J. (1997). Theories of Coping with Chronic Stress: Illustrations from the Health Psychology and Aging Literatures. In B.H. Gottlieb. (Ed.) *Coping with Chronic Stress*, (pp.75–103). New York: Plenum Press.

Antonovsky, A. (1979). *Health, Stress and Coping*. San Francisco: Jossey-Bass.

Antonucci, T. & Akiyama, H. (1987). Social networks in adult life and a preliminary examination of the convoy model, *Journal of Gerontology*, 45. 519–527.

Blazer, D. (1978). The Durham survey: description and application. *In Multidimensional Functional Assessment-the OARS Methodology: A Manual.* (2nd. Ed.). Duke University Center for the Study of Aging and Human Development, Durham, NC.

Chodoff, P. (1966). Effects of Extreme Coercive and Oppressive Forces: Brainwashing and Concentration Camps. In S. Arieti (Ed.), *American Handbook of Psychiatry, III*, (pp. 384–405). New York: Basic Books.

Friedman, M., & Rosenman, R. H. (1974). *Type A Behavior and Your Heart.* New York: Knopf.

Gottlieb, B.H. (1997). *Coping with Chronic Stress.* New York: Plenum Press.

Harel, Z., & Deimling, G. (1984) Social resources and mental health: an empirical refinement. *Journal of Gerontology*, 39, 747–752.

Harel, Z., Noelker, L., Blobe, B.F. (1985). Comprehensive services for the aged: Theoretical and empirical perspectives, *Gerontologist*, 25(6): 644–649.

Hyer, L. & Sohnle, S. (2001). *Trauma Among Older People: Issues in Treatment.* Philadelphia, PA: Brunner-Routledge.

Kahana, E., Fairchild T., & Kahana B. (1982). Adaptation. In D. J. Mangen & W.A. Peterson (Eds.), *Research Instruments in Social Gerontology: Clinical and Social Psychology* (pp.145–193). Minneapolis: University of Minnesota Press.

Kahana, B., Harel Z., & Kahana E. (1982). *Mental Health Implications of Extreme Stress for Late Life.* NIMH 1 ROl MH37714-01.

Kahana, E., Kahana B., Harel, Z. & Rosner, T. (1988). Coping with Extreme Trauma. In J. P. Wilson, Z. Harel & B. Kahana (Eds.), *Human Adaptation to Extreme Stress: From the Holocaust to Vietnam*, (pp.55–79). New York: Plenum Press.

Kahana, B., Harel, Z., & Kahana E. (1988). Predictors of Psychological Well Being Among Survivors of the Holocaust. In J. P. Wilson, Z. Harel & B. Kahana (Eds.). *Human Adaptation to Extreme Stress: From the Holocaust to Vietnam*, (pp.171–192). New York: Plenum.

Kahana, E. & Kahana, B. (2001). Holocaust Trauma and Sequelae. In E. Gerrity, T. Keane, & F. Tuma (Eds.) *The Mental Health Consequences of Torture*, (pp.143–158). New York: Kluwer Academic/Plenum Publishers.

Kasl, S. (1996) Theory of Stress and Health. In C. Cooper (Ed.). *Handbook of Stress. Medicine, and Health* (pp. 13–26). Boca Raton: CRC Press.

Larson, R., (1978). Thirty years of research on the subjective well-being of older Americans, *Journal of Gerontology*, 33, 109–129.

Lawton, M. P. (1975). The Philadelphia Geriatric Center morale scale: A revision. *Journal of Gerontology*, 30 85–89.

Lazarus, R. S. & Folkman (1984). *Stress, Appraisal and Coping.* New York: Springer.

Palmore, J. (1979). Predictors of successful aging, *The Gerontologist*, 19, 427–431.

Shanan, J. (1989). Surviving the survivors: Late personality development of Jewish Holocaust survivors, *International Journal of Mental Health*, 17, 42–71.

Shmotkin, D. & Lomrantz, J. (1998). Subjective well being among Holocaust survivors: An examination of overlooked differentiations, *Journal of Personality and Social Psychology*, 75, 141–155.

Weinfeld, M., Sigal, J. & Eaton, W. (1981). Long-term effects of the Holocaust on selected social attitudes and behaviors of survivors: A cautionary note, *Social Forces*, 60(1), 1–19.

Wrightsman, L. S. (1974). *Assumptions About Human Nature: A Social Psychological Approach.* Monterey, CA: Brooks/Cole Publishing Co. Inc.

9

Vulnerability, Resilience, Memories, and Meaning

In prior chapters of our book we sought to delineate physical and mental health, social supports and coping resources among Holocaust survivors and a comparison group of immigrants. We also sought to understand how personal and social resources and quality of life outcomes are interrelated among aging survivors participating in our research. We noted typologies of adaptation to the aging process among the highly traumatized Holocaust survivors and the less traumatized immigrants who nevertheless experienced the stressors of being refugees, fleeing countries where threats of the Holocaust provided the impetus for escaping. Furthermore, we considered differential adaptations and long-term outcomes among those survivors and those immigrants living in the U.S. as compared to those who had migrated to Israel. In addition to employing social science methodologies of survey research, we also sought to give voice to our respondents regarding their experiences, anchored in the historical periods and social milieus in which they occurred.

In this final chapter of our book, we are attempting to make sense of the complex data we presented. We link our prior discussion to broader theoretical understandings which can point the way to future research. We also briefly touch on implications of our research for clinical practice with trauma survivors.

VULNERABILITY AND RESILIENCE

The dual themes which emerge from our research are those which reflect divergent perspectives of the prior literature on Holocaust survivors in particular, and trauma survivors in general. The early, and particularly the clinical literature on Holocaust survivors focused almost exclusively on vulnerability, particularly in terms of impaired physical and mental health among survivors (Chodoff, 1963; Krystal, 1969; Danieli, 1988). In contrast, the more recent social science based research using community-based samples has emphasized resilience (Helmerich, 1992; Hass, 1990; Tedeschi, Crystal, & Lawrence, 1988).

Our data lend some support to each of these positions. By considering physical, psychological, and social functioning of survivors, we find evidence of both vulnerability and of resilience. In particular, vulnerability is demonstrated in areas of physical health (Trappler, Braunstein, & Moskowitz, 2002) and psychological well-being (Amir & Lev-Wiesel, 2003). However, there is notable overlap in the distribution between the survivors and the immigrant comparison group. Evidence of resilience is manifested primarily in social functioning and achievements of survivors. We also see resilience in the endorsement and transmission of humanitarian values and in commitments to bearing witness to the Holocaust, with the explicit purpose of protecting humankind from repeated acts of genocide or experiences of inhumanity (Shmotkin, Blumstein, & Modan, 2003).

Furthermore, our study calls attention to the need for looking beyond simple associations between trauma and vulnerability, or trauma and resilience. We are led to realize that there are diverse typologies of coping and aging in the aftermath of the Holocaust (Kahana, Kahana, Harel, Kahana, King, & Lovegreen, 1998). Future studies could benefit from looking for nonlinear patterns and from seeking to differentiate those survivors who exhibit resilience. We can also improve our understanding by considering how recent life events may lead to conditional vulnerability. Such patterns have been observed by other researchers as they considered responses of Holocaust survivors to other cases of collective or individual trauma, such as the scud missile crisis in Israel (Solomon, 1995) or older people facing individual trauma such as diagnosis of cancer (Deimling, Kahana, Bowman, & Schaefer, 2002).

Moving beyond our observations of the long-term sequelae of having lived through the extreme trauma of the Holocaust, we are still left with important questions about the processes which may explain resilience of survivors. A variety of explanations have been proposed to account for the relative absence of adverse outcomes among long-term survivors of extreme trauma. One explanation relates to selective long-term survival of those with the greatest resiliency and personality resources prior to the trauma (Antonovsky & Sagy, 1986). A second explanation relates to the inoculation effect of extreme stress, which results in greater hardiness among those facing stressors subsequent to trauma (Kobasa, Maddi, Puccett, & Zola, 1994). It may also be argued that survivors were aided by supportive personal, social, and cultural environments, which buffered the ill effects of trauma (Kahana & Kahana, 2003). Finally, positive long-term outcomes may also be attributed to the healing process, which improves well being subsequent to trauma. Clinical psychologists may attribute these to the regenerative powers of the ego (Rappaport, 1968) whereas sociologists or social psychologists point to the importance of social integration and support (Kahana, Kahana, Harel, & Rosner, 1988).

Exploring New Directions

Having provided a brief analysis of major study findings, we must venture beyond theoretical questions explicitly addressed by our study and point to some previously neglected conceptual areas suggested by our research, which should be explored in future studies. Two such areas with potential heuristic value are linked lives and community context.

Linked Lives

The concept of linked lives, which is central to life course studies (Elder, 1987), emphasizes the important connection of individuals moving through the life course to significant others to whom they may be linked by deep attachments or by shared experiences. This concept has been implicitly noted in the literature on the Holocaust, but has not been explicitly conceptualized and studied. It is important to note that most survivors emerged from normal and loving families, where their early lives had been positively linked with those of their parents, siblings, and extended family members. This is illustrated in our data where the vast majority of survivors describe their prewar family environment as warm and loving. Coming from close families with strong and cohesive values, our respondents moved into the horrors where all human linkages were disrupted and broken.

To the extent that we can seriously recognize the importance of linked lives, the brutal separations from one's closest kin, and even the witnessing of the murder of those closest to an individual underscore the ultimate socioemotional disruptions that most survivors experienced. Yet, notwithstanding the horrors endured by survivors, the supreme importance of social ties re-emerged during the trauma as people valiantly struggled to help fellow victims or to protect those close to them in Ghettos and camps (Kahana, Kahana, Harel, & Segall, 1986; Tec, 2003).

In the aftermath of the Holocaust, linked lives once again emerged as a path to redemption. Survivors married, raised new or first families, and their families assumed supreme significance and closeness. We found that survivors in our research established very close ties with their families of procreation, with 98% of the U.S. sample having married and only 2% ever having been divorced or separated. We can thus relate the experience of the Holocaust survivors to notions of Elder (1987) about the ways in which social forces shape the life course and its developmental consequences.

Survivors in our study lived through devastating experiences in enduring man's inhumanity to man. Fitting in with Raphael's (1986) notion that disasters create disruption in normal coping responses, survivors in our study were clearly psychologically scarred. Their prior trust in authority, in predictability, and in society, had been shaken. Nevertheless, amazingly, their values had remained mostly intact. For most survivors, an overlay of hope could co-exist with mistrust (Kahana, Kahana, Harel, Kelly, Monaghan, & Holland, 1997). The literature generally concludes that the adverse sequelae of surviving unspeakable horrors result in intergenerational transmission of trauma (Hass, 1990, Felsen, 1998). Nonetheless, there is also, triumph in survivors' ability to link their lives to the next generation through intergenerational transmission of values (Kahana & Kahana, 2001).

Community Context

Most studies of Holocaust survivorship have documented the individual sequelae of having been traumatized by society. An important lesson from our study is the powerful influence of the social context through the pre-traumatic past, experience of the trauma, and survivorship. Holocaust survivors had started their lives as members of closely-knit communities, with shared religious and cultural symbols. For many, the horrors of the Holocaust were endured in "communities of horror", in ghettos and concentration camps where they were surrounded by other victims, forming a surrealistic community of victims. Even those who survived as part of the resistance movement were embedded in a closely-knit small community of other resistance fighters. Of course, there are exceptions to this notion of community for those who survived in hiding or with false papers.

Community influences were once again discernable after the Holocaust, as survivors' experiences were shaped by needing to acculturate and become part of new communities, learning new languages, social norms, and expectations. While our research is based on those survivors who migrated to the U.S. and to Israel, we must also note that some survivors continued to live in the communities where atrocities had been perpetrated against them and against members of their family (e.g., survivors remaining in Hungary).

The influence of society, broadly defined, and community, more narrowly construed, on a survivor's experiences has seldom been the subject of systematic inquiry. Our study afforded the opportunity to look at differences in post-traumatic adaptations of survivors who relocated to Israel and those who immigrated to the U.S. Our initial hypothesis had been that persons residing in Israel, a war-torn and relatively poor country fighting for independence, would exhibit more distress in the aftermath of the Holocaust than those fortunate to immigrate to the U.S., an affluent and peaceful land. It was surprising to find that stressfulness of the community environment did not turn out to be its most important feature in influencing the well-being of survivors or that of the immigrants in our research. Contrary to our expectations, survivors living in Israel exhibited better psychological adaptations than those living in the U.S. (Harel, Kahana, & Kahana, 1988) Survivors living in Israel felt less isolated and stigmatized and more trustful of their fellow citizens than those living in the U.S. (Kahana et al., 1997). It may have been indeed the opportunity to observe and to participate in the establishment of their homeland, the State of Israel, that accounted for relative psychological well being. These findings, while descriptive and not causally linked, suggest the special importance of social integration for trauma survivors.

It is within this important community context that we must look at the individual survivors as the protagonists rather than just the reactors (George, 1998). Thus, we learn from survivors' accounts of their life story, that fifty years after the original trauma, many were able to move from helpless victims to active "story tellers" (Wolfenstein, 1957). By listening to stories of survivors, society helps to reduce their isolation. Those who did not endure the Holocaust can also make a contribution by making an effort to learn from survivors, even if they can't comprehend the horrors that these individuals have been through (Hass, 1996). It is only through listening to stories of survivors that we, as a society, can move from denial to recognition of the possibility of evil. By listening to survivors, we can also stop blaming the victims (Solomon, 1995). By seeking to understand society's ultimate responsibility for the evils that victimized survivors in the past we can take active steps to reduce the occurrence of such evils in the future.

FINDING FULFILLMENT IN THE AFTERMATH OF TRAUMA

Based on in-depth interviews with Holocaust survivors, Hass (1996) has called attention to their valiant efforts at keeping the past at bay. He argues that the arduous process at normalization can only be achieved by "compartmentalizing" their Holocaust experiences. Thus, survivors are notably successful in terms of social achievements, and take pride in those achievements. In spite of intrusive memories of trauma, the overwhelming majority of survivors view themselves as "normal" and "happy" with their success in rebuilding their lives. What eludes many of them, however, is a sense of inner peace, and they live eternally vigilant as they try to keep their traumatic memories from surfacing.

These observations are consistent with data from our research and they suggest that the underlying anguish of the trauma endured cannot fully heal (Kahana et al., 1997). However, our emphasis in this book is on the remarkable success of coping efforts on the part of this severely traumatized population. By acknowledging components of losses in survivors' quality of life as well as their transcendent values and achievements, we can insure that we will never minimize the inhumanity of their past, but also we will extol the triumph of their spirit.

Many Holocaust survivors cannot fully enjoy happy occasions. This characteristic of survivors has been defined by clinicians to constitute a traumatic neurosis termed "alexithymia" (Krystal & Krystal, 1988). But, looking at survivors' difficulty to experience joy, there is the palpable absence of families of orientation, the very people with whom one can normally share one's joys. Furthermore, it may be argued that fully experiencing joy, that so many of one's fellow Jews never lived to see, would be an insult to their memory. There is no one who can grant permission to survivors to be carefree (Hass, 1996). Survivors must always find a purpose to compensate for their collective loss. Good works, helping others, or other forms of constructive engagement can thus help compensate for survivors' inability to fully enjoy life if they are still haunted by memories of loss.

As survivors of the Holocaust are now elderly and diminishing in numbers, opportunities to study this group are also becoming increasingly scarce. The psychological scars left on survivors and even the problems that some of their offspring confront have been extensively documented (Danieli, 1984; Tec, 2003). We believe that our research has also provided us with the opportunity to consider the psychological strengths that have enabled survivors to rebuild their lives and achieve a measure of integration.

We found that these strengths derived from several typologies of new meaning. These include: (1) establishing, raising, and nurturing families of procreation; (2) establishing successful work and professional lives; (3) establishing and nurturing associations of Holocaust survivors for honoring and keeping collective memories of the Holocaust alive (4) engaging in religious and humanitarian pursuits and (5) supporting and contributing to the survival of the Jewish community and to building a homeland in the State of Israel.

IMPLICATIONS FOR PRACTICE, THERAPY, AND SERVICES

In the fields of health and human services, assumptions made about the nature and needs of service consumers determine practice objectives.

Beliefs held by professionals about the nature and needs of individuals and groups have also determined treatment strategies, and care practices (Harel, Kahana, & Kahana, 1984). For this reason, the exploration of perceptions held about the Holocaust and of Holocaust survivors by members of various professional groups and by survivors themselves is important (Pearlman & Saakvitne, 1995). A better comprehension and understanding of the diversity of Holocaust survivors by professionals is likely to enhance their ability to serve and represent the survivors' interests and needs (Kahana et al., 1998).

Similarities in perceptions are likely to facilitate meaningful communications between survivors and professionals who help them. Contradictory perceptions and/or misguided assumptions by professionals about the nature and needs of individuals and families seeking professional help are likely to lead to mistrust and alienation and hinder relationships which in turn, impede the delivery of effective services (Wilson & Thomas, 2004). Survivors seeking professional help need the assurance of professional sensitivity and understanding to their concerns and needs. Survivors' perceptions that the individual practitioners and members of the professional community are understanding and respectful of their sufferings, losses, and painful memories should enhance the ability of professionals to serve clients who are survivors. Therefore, the therapists' understanding of mental health implications of extreme stress for survivors is important (Ochberg, 1993).

Practice efforts of health and human service professionals need to be guided by one or more of the following objectives: a) provide older individuals and families with effective services that are efficiently delivered; b) allow older Holocaust survivors as much discretion as possible over the services they use; c) encourage and support family members and friends in caring for survivors in need of attention and assistance and d) enhance the coping resources of older Holocaust survivors and members of their informal caregivers (Harel, Noelker, & Blake, 1985). These objectives are important in working with all elderly to help reduce vulnerabilities and are applicable to professionals working with people who endured traumatic stress in their lives.

Health and human service professionals need to direct their efforts to help Holocaust survivors deal as constructively as possible with the psychological implications of their earlier traumatic experiences and social losses and to aid their current adjustment (Wilson & Thomas, 2004). In addition to formal interventions of psychotherapists' informal support can be a valuable adjunct and, for some, even substitute for formal treatment.

Although there are very clear differences between situations of extreme stress, these experiences all place extraordinary demands on aging survivors who are forced to cope both with the consequences of the intense trauma they endured and the challenges that come with old age, such as declining health or loss of friends and relatives. Currently, we have limited understandings concerning sensitive and appropriate forms of therapy and support for survivors of extreme stress. It is important to acknowledge that many of the treatment approaches for trauma survivors have limited empirical bases (Wilson, Harel, & Kahana, 1988).

The distress of the survivor may often be shared in empathetic ways by the therapist who has the responsibility to listen in non-judgmental ways about some of the most cruel, hideous and tortuous experiences that humans have inflicted on their fellow humans. The severity of the experiences may, at times, create unique problems of counter-transference in the therapist and may pose added challenges in their practice (Danieli, 1988).

There is an ever present dynamic tension between the survivor's need to forget and the need to remember. There is also a particular vulnerability to loss and separation (Kahana et al., 1997). Illness, hospitalization, institutionalization, social losses, and other life stresses may reawaken earlier stress- related feelings of regimentation, helplessness, and powerlessness. Among Holocaust survivors, the recognition of the collective meaning of their experiences is very important. Working with survivors of extreme stress is challenging, difficult, and emotionally taxing. And yet, it must be kept in perspective that models for treatment of older survivors of extreme stress are only useful if they aid their adjustment to current challenges and to consequences of their earlier stressful experiences.

Like other older persons, Holocaust survivors need to be respected within their social networks and associations. Participation in social support networks is not only important for the availability of care in times of need, but also appears to promote better mental health.

CONSIDERATIONS FOR COLLECTIVE MEMORY

As genocides and other atrocities toward human beings continue to occur around the world, searching for lessons from the Nazi Holocaust continues to pose important challenges to scholars (Markusen, 1993; Bauer, 1982). It is only in recent times that, in considering the Holocaust, scholars have expanded their orientation to encompass not only perpetrators and victims, but also bystanders (Hilberg, 1992). Thus, there is a growing recognition that multiple perspectives must be considered to fully appreciate the complexity of this catastrophe.

The literature on the Holocaust may be approached from the vantage points of many disciplines, with publications ranging from historical and philosophical treatises to eyewitness accounts and clinical studies (Rosenberg & Myers, 1988). More recently, there has also been an increase in empirical community studies by psychologists and sociologists (Helmreich, 1992; Shmotkin & Lomranz, 1998; Kahana & Kahana, 2001). Only recently has the literature begun to pay attention to potential differences in the assumptions made by those approaching the Holocaust from different vantage points and are seeing genocide and its collective memories through different prisms (Midlarsky, 2005).

In focusing on the Holocaust during the last twenty years in the United States, there has been growing attention to this tragic period in European history, with Holocaust memorials being erected and curricula about the Holocaust increasingly taught across the U.S. (Meyers, 2002). At the same time, academic observers have also been interested, and at times baffled by the meaning of this belated focus on the Holocaust as a manifestation of collective memory. Some authors aim to minimize the importance of deriving lessons from the Holocaust.

In his controversial book, *The Holocaust in American Life*, Novick (1999) argues that there are no useful lessons to be learned from the Holocaust and that collective memory in the case of the Holocaust is a function of political agendas, independent of the historical facts or moral indignation about genocide. Pulitzer Prize-winning author Kakutani (1999) characterizes this view as deliberate cynicism.

Remembering the Holocaust or other great human-made disasters for the future is a holistic enterprise that cannot be placed in an abstract sphere and than taken away from the victims, from those who care about the victims or those who want to carry on their legacy (Tanay, 2004). Survivors and their descendents carry not only the residue of trauma but also the visceral indignation about the perpetration of evil, which often eludes academic analyses. Participation in academic conferences helped us and fellow survivors to understand that we mustn't be afraid to feel, because feelings humanize our experiences and can clarify the importance of memories. Lack of feelings, as reflected in cold objectivity, can lead to loss of compassion and to cynicism that distances reality. We must not forget that perpetrators of the Holocaust were often accomplished scientists who developed clever and evil theories (Lifton & Markusen, 1988) and sophisticated means of destruction. They succeeded in their nefarious goals because of lack of feelings and compassion for human dignity and human life among both bystanders and perpetrators.

Yes, we need museums, memorials, and Holocaust curricula. We need psychologists to study post-traumatic stress (Danieli, 1997) and historians to confront Holocaust deniers (Lipstadt, 1994). Some academics raise concern about the risks that we may stop remembering. Alternatively, they wonder whether it is important for the future, to make concerted efforts to remember. From the vantage point of survivors, the reasons for remembering are simple, clearly necessary and should be understandable for all. Remembering, for survivors, relates to honoring the memories of the millions of human beings who were murdered, and who were not allowed the opportunity to complete their lives and leave legacies. We need to remember what was done to them. Thus, all mankind may know about the perpetration of this great inhuman atrocity. We need to remember this so that future generations can learn to resist evil.

Future research must consider both conflicts and areas of convergence in the perspectives of survivors and those connected to them, anchored in experiential reality and the abstract perspectives of academics. Here we may echo Emile Fackenheim's (1994) views that understanding of collective memories may be easier through the common sense lenses of survivors than through the allegedly "sophisticated models" of academic disciplines.

It has taken the world over fifty years to assimilate the meaning of the Holocaust. Perhaps the time has also come for survivors' voices to be heard and listened to by the academic establishment. Survivors need to participate in future efforts to memorialize the Holocaust and other manmade disasters, including September 11th, 2001. Survivors are valuable as advisors, role models, and repositories of "memory", rather than only as damaged human specimens, reflecting the trauma. Remembering involves personal "time travel" to the memories in question. Academic discourse typically involves abstractions, which take us outside the domain of memory. Survivors are the ones who can literally remember. They must inform and challenge the intellectual discourse on legacies of the Holocaust. Their memories hold the key not only to their trauma but also to their survival. Uncommon experiences and survival have endowed survivors with keen common sense.

As time elapses, there are fewer and fewer survivors to bring authenticity to conversation about the Holocaust. Therefore, it is ever more important that we consider survivor perspectives. Survivors can help academics recognize that their jargon often hides the immediacy of life and of human experience (Adorno, 1973). The Holocaust represents a universal symbol of human suffering, inflicted by and acquiesced to by multitudes of otherwise civilized people. Awareness that we must remember, feel, and act in the face of all human suffering is a timely message learned from survivors. Scientific analysts of the Holocaust and of other trauma must be reminded that they cannot bring indifference to human suffering (Wiesel, 1987). We should not tolerate speaking about other people's suffering without requisite emotions. The study of genocide cannot be morally neutral. It must always encompass concern with caring and the human spirit. Those who both feel and remember can contribute in important ways to help build collective memories worth remembering (Langer, 1991). Academics can also make important contributions to humanistic discourse, which treats trauma in its full social context. It is our collective responsibility, as a society, to confront indifference so we can always collectively feel and remember. This will help not only the survivors of the Holocaust and their descendents, but all humankind.

REFERENCES

Adorno, T. (1973). *Negative Dialects, translated by E.B. Ashton.* New York: Seabury Press.

Amir, M., & Lev-Wiesel, R. (2003). Time does not heal all wounds: Quality of life and psychological distress of people who survived the Holocaust as children 55 years later, *Journal of Traumatic Stress*, 16(3): 295–299.

Antonovsky, H., & Sagy, S. (1986). The development of a sense of coherence and its impact on responses to stress situations, *Journal of Social Psychology*, 126(2): 213–225.

Bauer, Y. (1982). *A History of the Holocaust.* New York: Franklin Watts.

Chodoff, P. (1963). Late effects of the concentration camp syndrome. *Archives of General Psychiatry*, Apr., 323–333.

Danieli, Y. (1984). Psychotherapists' participation in the conspiracy of silence about the Holocaust, *Psychoanalytic Psychology*, 1(1): 23–42.

Danieli, Y. (1988). *Treating Survivors and Children of Survivors of the Nazi Holocaust.* New York, N.Y.: Bruner Mazel.

Danieli, Y. (1997). As survivors age: an overview. *Journal of Geriatric Psychiatry*, 30(1), 9–26.

Deimling, G.T., Kahana, B., Bowman, K.F., & Schaefer, M.L. (2002). Cancer survivorship and psychological distress in later life, *Psycho-Oncology*, 11 (6): 479–494.

Elder, G.H. Jr. (1987). Families and lives: some developments in life course studies, *Journal of Family History*, 12(1–3): 179–199.

Fackenheim, E.L. (1994). *To Mend the World: Foundations of Post-Holocaust Jewish Thought.* Bloomington, IN: Indiana University Press, Reprint Edition.

Felsen, I. (1998). Transgenerational Transmission of Effects of the Holocaust: The North American Research Perspective. In Y. Danieli (Ed.). *International Handbook of Multigenerational Legacies of Trauma* (43–68). New York, NY: Plenum Press.

George, L. (1998). Dignity and quality of life in old age, *Journal of Gerontological Social Work*, 29 (2–3): 39–52.

Harel, Z., Kahana, B. & Kahana, E. (1984). Psychiatric, Behavioral Science and Survivor Perspectives on the Holocaust. *Journal of Sociology and Social Welfare.* XI, 915–929.

Harel, Z., Noelker, L. & Blake, B. (1985). Planning services for the aged: Theoretical and empirical perspectives. *Gerontologist*, 25: 644–649.

Harel, Z., Kahana, B. & Kahana, E. (1988). Psychological well-being among survivors of the Holocaust in Israel. *Journal of Traumatic Stress Studies I*, 413–429.

Hass, A. (1990). *In the Shadow of the Holocaust: The Second Generation.* New York: Cambridge University Press.

Hass, A. (1995). *The Aftermath: Living with the Holocaust.* New York: Cambridge University Press.

Helmreich, W. (1992). *Against all odds: Holocaust survivors and the successful lives they made in America.* New York, NY: Simon & Schuster.

Hass, A. (1996). *The Aftermath: Living with the Holocaust.* New York: Cambridge University Press.

Hillberg, R. (1992). *Perpetrators, Victims, Bystanders: The Jewish Catastrophe 1933–1945.* New York: Aaron Asher Books.

Kahana, B., Kahana, E., Harel, Z., & Segall, M. (1986). The victim as helper: prosocial behavior during the Holocaust. *Humboldt Journal of Social Relations,* 13 (1&2): 357–373.

Kahana, E., Kahana, B., Harel, Z., & Rosner, T. (1988). Coping With Extreme Trauma. In J. Wilson, Z. Harel, & B. Kahana (Eds.), *Human Adaptation to Extreme Stress: From the Holocaust to Vietnam* (pp. 55–79). New York, NY: Plenum Publishing Co.

Kahana, B., Kahana, E., Harel, Z., Kelly, K., Monaghan, P., & Holland, L. (1997). A Framework for Understanding the Chronic Stress of Holocaust Survivors. In M. Gottlieb (Ed.), *Coping with Chronic Stress* (pp. 315–342). New York, NY: Plenum Publishing Co.

Kahana, E., Kahana, B., Harel, H., Kahana, M., King, C., & Lovegreen, L. (1998, November). *Survivors of the Nazi Holocaust face old age.* Paper presented at the 51st Annual Meeting of the Gerontological Society of America, Philadelphia, PA.

Kahana, B. & Kahana, E. (2001). Holocaust Trauma and Sequelae. In E. Gerrity, T. Keane, & F. Tuma (Eds.) *The Mental Health Consequences of Torture.* New York: Kluwer Academic/Plenum Publishers.

Kahana, E., & Kahana, B. (2003). Contextualizing Successful Aging: New Directions in Age-Old Search. In R. Settersten, Jr. (Ed.), *Invitation to the Life Course: A New Look at Old Age* (pp. 225–255). Amityville, NY: Baywood Publishing Company.

Kakutani, M. (August, 17, 1999, Book Review). *Books of the Times: Taking Aim at the Symbolism of the Holocaust.* New York Times. The Holocaust in American Life, by Peter Novick. Houghton Mifflin Company.

Kobasa, S.C., Maddi, S.R., Puccett, M.C., & Zola, M.A. (1995). Effectiveness of Hardiness, Exercise and Social Support as Resources Against Illness. In A. Steptoe and J. Wardle (Eds.). *Psychosocial Processes and Health: A Reader.* New York: Cambridge U. Press.

Krystal, H. (1969). *Massive Psychic Trauma.* New York: International Universities Press.

Krystal, H. & Krystal, J. (1988). *Integration and Self Healing: Affect, Trauma, Alexithymia.* Hillsdale, N.J.: Analytic Press.

Langer, L.L. (1993). *Holocaust Testimonies: The Ruins of Memory.* New Haven: Yale University Press.

Lifton, R.J. & Markusen, E. (1990). *The Genocidal Mentality: Nazi Holocaust and Nuclear Threat.* New York: Basic Books, Inc.

Lipstadt, D.E. (1994). *Denying the Holocaust: The Growing Assault on Truth and Memory.* New York, NY: Free Press.

Markusen, E. (1993). Lessons and Legacies: The Meaning of the Holocaust in a Changing World. In Y. Bauer & H. Locke (Eds.), *Holocaust and Genocide Studies.* Oxford, England: Oxford University Press, 263–273.

Meyers, P.A. (2002). The Holocaust in American life. *European Journal of Social Theory,* 5(1): 149–164.

Midlarsky, M. (2005). *The Killing Fields.* New York: Cambridge University Press.

Novick, P. (1999). *The Holocaust in American Life.* Boston: Houghton Mifflin.

Ochberg, F.M. (1993). Posttraumatic Therapy. In J.P. Wilson, B. Raphael (Eds.), *International Handbook of Traumatic Stress Syndromes.* New York, NY: Plenum Press, 773–785.

Pearlman, L. & Saakvitne, K. (1995). *Trauma and the Therapist.* New York: Norton.

Raphael, B. (1986). *When Disaster Strikes: How Individuals and Communities Cope with Catastrophe.* New York: Basic Books.

Rappaport, E. (1968). Beyond traumatic neurosis: A psychoanalytic study of late reactions to concentration camp trauma. *International Journal of Psycho-Analysis,* 49(4), 719–731.

Rosenberg, A. & Myers, G.E. (1988). *Echoes From the Holocaust: Philosophical Reflections on a Dark Time.* Philadelphia: Temple University Press.

Shmotkin, D., & Lomranz, J. (1998). Subjective well-being among Holocaust survivors: An examination of overlooked differentiations, *Journal of Personality and Social Psychology,* 75: 141–155.

Shmotkin, D., Blumstein, T., & Modan, B. (2003). Tracing the long-term effects of early trauma: A broad-scope view of Holocaust survivors in late life, *Journal of Consulting and Clinical Psychology*, 71(2): 223–234.

Solomon, Z. (1995). From denial to recognition: Attitudes towards Holocaust survivors from WW II to the present. *Journal of Traumatic Stress, 8 (2), 2–15.*

Tanay, E. (2004). Passport to Life: Autobiographical Reflections on the Holocaust. Ann Arbor, Michigan: Forensic Press.

Tec, N. (2003). *Resilience and Courage.* New Haven, CT: Yale University Press.

Tedeschi, R., Crystal L. P., & Lawrence G. C. (1988). *Posttraumatic Growth: Positive Changes in the Aftermath of Crisis.* Lawrence Erlbaum Associates, Inc: Mahwah, N.J.

Thomas, R. & Wison John P. (2004). Issues and Controversies in Understanding and Diagnosis of Compassion Fatigue, Vicarious Traumatization, and Secondary Traumatic Stress Disorder. *International Journal of Emergency Mental Health* Vol 6 (2), 81–92

Trappler, B., Braunstein, J., & Moskowitz, G. (2002). Holocaust survivors in a primary care setting: Fifty years later, *Psychological Reports*, 91, 545–552.

Wilson, J. Harel, Z. & Kahana, B. (Eds). (1988). *Human Adaptation to Extreme Stress: From Holocaust to Vietnam.* New York: Plenum Publishing Co.

Wiesel, E. (1987). *Twilight.* New York: Summit Books.

Wolfenstein, M. (1957). *Disaster: A Psychological Essay.* Illinois: Free Press.

Index